"Of all the people we have met and all the organizations we have encountered in ministry to those who want sexual sanctification, John Freeman and Harvest USA are the ones we trust. The fruit of John's experience in this book should be a help to many."

Tim Keller, Senior Pastor, Redeemer Presbyterian Church, New York, NY; author of *The Reason for God*

"We live in a hyper-sexualized culture, where porn is the norm and everyone is harmed by secret sexual sin. John Freeman is savvy about sexual temptation, sensitive to men who feel hopeless, and sold on the power of the gospel to bring real spiritual transformation. Before you give up hope for sexual healing, give *Hide or Seek* a chance to help bring the change you need."

Philip Ryken, President at Wheaton College

"John Freeman has written a book for men who are sexual strugglers—in other words, he has written a book for *all* men! John relentlessly applies the gospel—the love of God for us in Christ—to our sexual dysfunction. The gospel frees us to open up our lives both to our heavenly Father and to one another and begin the hard but good work of purity. John's gentle and generous heart jumps from the pages of this book and mirrors the heart of God for men who are struggling. Bridging the gap between theology and practice, this book is a call to biblical integrity, to wholeness, where the inner life matches the outer appearance."

Paul E. Miller, Director of seeJesus; author of *A Loving Life*

"When Christian men talk about sex, I either feel the weight of sin or I don't feel the weight of glory. This is not the case with John Freeman. Few hold the complexities of our struggle with sex with the compelling goodness of what God created. H ̶ ̶ ̶ ̶ ̶ ̶ ̶ l compelling and invites us to taste the ̶ ̶ ̶ ̶ ̶ ̶ ̶ kenness and holy longing."

Dan B. Allender, Ph ̶ ̶ ̶ ̶ ̶ ̶ **hology and** Founding President, ̶ ̶ ̶ ̶ ̶ ̶ ̶ **nd Psychol-** ogy; author of *The Wou̶ ̶ ̶ ̶ ̶ ̶ Heart*

"Here is what you will appreciate about John's book: It's the fruit of the work he has done in helping men for over thirty years. He was talking with men about sexual temptation while it was still taboo to make any sexual reference in most churches. You will find him to be an experienced, wise mentor who will guide you with both his words and his life."

Ed Welch, PhD, CCEF Faculty; psychologist; best-selling author

"An excellent, easily readable, down-to-earth, grace-filled, and compassionate journey into the world of men's struggle with pornography with a biblical diagnosis of the heart problems that lie behind the struggle and a prescription for hope and healing. John Freeman's long experience of helping men who struggle with sexual brokenness is revealed in many stories of pain and shame. His compassion and love is demonstrated in his desire to help them (and his readers) know the depths of the forgiveness, love, and grace of God. He weaves a narrative of personal experiences, others' stories, biblical character studies, and, finally, practical suggestions, to offer help on the road to discovering the truth about God and our need of his grace and help in breaking free from the chains of sexual slavery."

Richard Winter, MD, Psychotherapist and Professor of Practical Theology and Counseling at Covenant Theological Seminary, St. Louis, MO

"Most books written to men with sexual problems leave readers feeling hopeless—hopeless because they feel shamed by the author or unsure if the 'simple' steps offered really work. Sometimes strugglers fear picking up a book like this for fear they will only feel worse when done. If that is you, I encourage you to pick up this book and to read slowly. On these pages John Freeman communicates something better than more shame and hopelessness. He exudes honesty and clarity about the nature of sexual struggles but in love, compassion, and hope for your present and future. As you read, you will know that John understands your sexual struggles, believes that you do not need to 'slink back to the cross,' and paints a picture of hope in coming out of the fog."

Philip G. Monroe, PsyD, Professor of Counseling & Psychology at Biblical Seminary Graduate School of Counseling

"Finally, John's book is out! For over a decade I've longed for the day when John Freeman's love for the gospel, understanding of sexual brokenness, and compassionate heart would converge in printed form, and *Hide or Seek* is everything I hoped it would be. In over thirty-five years of ordained ministry, I've never met anyone with a better grasp of the spiritual issues, care-giving considerations, family dynamics, and the healing journey for those of us struggling with sexual brokenness than John. As a pastor, I have seen firsthand the fruit of John's ministry, and that of Harvest USA. If you read this book, you will most definitely buy more for others."

    Scotty Smith, Founding Pastor of Christ Community Church; Teacher in Residence at West End Community Church; author of *Everyday Prayers: 365 Days to a Gospel-Centered Faith*

"The last time we had John Freeman on the daily radio program (HAVEN Today) I lead, we had to offer an alternative program to the most listened-to Christian teaching/talk radio station in America. The station founder and the pastor of one of America's most well-known churches would not allow the word 'sex' to be used on his airtime. Thankfully, that time has passed and, thankfully, John has written *Hide or Seek* . . . a book that addresses the biggest problem we face in the Christian world today. While primarily written to men, this book is long overdue and it speaks to women and men. If you subscribe to Sola Scriptura as I do, how can we not address the hidden sin that plagues all of us? I needed this book of hope. We all do. It oozes with grace that we desperately need to not just find our hope in Christ alone, but to overcome by the power of the gospel. *Hide or Seek* reminds me once again that grace trumps everything."

    Charles Morris, President and Speaker of Haven Ministries

"John Freeman's *Hide or Seek: When Men Get Real with God About Sex* is an authentic look into the deepest struggles of masculine sexuality. It is a gift of hope to the Christian soul. Here you will find not just the sting of truth, but also the joy of grace, the light of wisdom, and the encouragement of a trusted counselor and friend. You need this book and so do the men in your life that you know and love."

    Dr. Peter A. Lillback, President, Westminster Theological Seminary, Philadelphia, PA

"John Freeman has succeeded! And, in my opinion, similar written attempts to help in this area of sexuality rarely do! How has he succeeded in a sea of noble but failed attempts? Here is my answer. If you ask yourself two questions I ask whenever I read a book like John's, you will see what I mean. First, how well does this book help me read and know my God and his Word? Second, how well does this book help me read and know myself? To be of any actual assistance, a work like this simply must do both—unveiling my King to me and unmasking myself to me. John's work succeeds on both counts very, very well. Now I warn you! John's work has a prophetic edge that cuts deep. It hurt as he showed me how I simultaneously need but resist the Holy Spirit's 'holy and wholly disruption!' Thanks, John. This book hurts like heaven which seems worse than hell, because heaven wants me to change and hell hopes I never do!"

Joe Novenson, Senior Pastor at Lookout Mountain Presbyterian Church, Lookout Mountain, TN

"John Freeman has written a good and important book. *Hide or Seek* is easy to read, but not easy to experience. I think John has been reading my mail, or should I say he makes it plain that God is reading our collective mail as sexual beings. If anyone has struggled with overwhelming sexual lust, pornography, adultery, or same-sex attraction, then you should read this book, and my prayer would be that you would find hope in the gospel and rest for your soul. This will be a book that many pastors will not only want to have and read, but a book they will want to give away to those coming to them for help as they cry out for deliverance from sexual bondage."

Randy Nabors, Pastor Emeritus, New City Fellowship (PCA)

HIDE OR SEEK

WHEN MEN GET REAL WITH GOD ABOUT SEX

John Freeman

New
Growth
Press

www.newgrowthpress.com

New Growth Press, Greensboro, NC 27404
Copyright © 2014 by Harvest USA

Cover Design: Faceout Books, faceoutstudio.com
Typesetting and eBook: Lisa Parnell, lparnell.com

ISBN 978-1-939946-63-8 (Print)
ISBN 978-1-939946-64-5 (eBook)

Library of Congress Cataloging-in-Publication Data
Freeman, John, 1953–
 Hide or seek : when men get real with God about sex / John Freeman.
  pages cm
 ISBN 978-1-939946-63-8 (print : alk. paper) — ISBN 978-1-939946-64-5 (ebook)
 1. Sex—Religious aspects—Christianity. 2. Christian men—Sexual behavior.
 I. Title.
 BT708.F74 2014
 241'.6640811—dc23
                                                                2014016282

Printed in the United States of America

21 20 19 18 17 16 15 14   1 2 3 4 5

This book is dedicated to Ingrid, Eileen,
Carolyn, Barbara (my mom)—and to my wife, Penny.
As five godly women whose love and support
have helped me be the man I am and hope to be,
they, each in their own unique way,
have been precious gifts of God.

Contents

Foreword

A number of years ago, my friend Harold Myra wrote a little book, *Is There a Place I Can Scream?* It is an incredibly authentic book of colloquial prayers dealing with difficult issues. One prayer/poem called "Jet Sex Engine" poses the question: "Why did God put a jet sex engine in my Volkswagen body?"

Good question. I've asked that same sort of question myself.

Our sexuality and sexual desires are complicated, confusing, and a mix of joy, fear, and guilt. Not only that, they are powerful—so powerful that they are at the heart of how we define ourselves. Most studies show that we all spend a considerable amount of our time thinking about sex, fantasizing about it, and wondering about it, and then trying to pretend we aren't.

If you've never asked why God made our sexuality so powerful or why we all struggle with our sexuality, then this isn't your book. If you've never made promises about your sexuality you couldn't keep, worked to put some brakes on your lust you couldn't pull off, tried to "put it out of your mind" without success, or tried to rationalize your sexual desires knowing that rationalization was nonsense, you may be living as an outsider to the human race or, alternatively, living with enough denial to skew everything else you think important. Be that as it may, take this book back to the seller and get your money back.

Christians have been doing that for a very long time—taking the book back, as it were, and pretending we're protecting our purity and that of our family and friends! But we are deceiving ourselves. Our lack of honesty about our sexuality is killing us and destroying our credibility. And more important, it's causing us to miss an amazing demonstration of Christ's love for us and the gifts of freedom and wholeness he would desire for his church and his people.

A while back, one of my students asked a pastor in his eighties when the struggle with lust got better. "Son," he said, laughing, "it doesn't get better until you're dead . . . and have been buried for at least a week."

Oh, yes it does!

It depends on how we define "getting better." If you define *getting better* as never having to struggle, living without wounds, and "tiptoeing through the garden with Jesus," you will end up being disappointed because that's not going to happen. But if you define *getting better* as walking in the light and "kissing the demons" so they lose their controlling power, then there is hope and good news in the gospel. If you define *getting better* as getting loved, forgiven, and free from the debilitating power of the lies, prevarications, and shallowness, this book has some very good news about *getting better*.

I don't care where your mind has gone, what you've watched on the Internet, with whom you've slept, what direction your desires have gone, how hard you've struggled and failed, whom you've hurt, or how ashamed you are. The good news is that, first, you haven't surprised the God who gave us the "jet sex engine" and, second, he's not angry at you but will show you a way to live in the light. Jack Miller used to say that the entire Bible could be summed up in two sentences: "Cheer up, you're a lot worse than you think you are. And cheer up, God's grace is a lot bigger than you think it is."

I'm a cynical, old preacher who is less cynical because of John Freeman. He's been my friend for a whole lot of years and I've watched him speak truth when people didn't want to hear it, love people others would rather avoid, and stand in the gap that many Christians didn't even think exists.

We can't do that anymore. We've got to talk. We've got to talk about sex.

That's what this book is about. What you will read here is honest, true, refreshing, and so important and insightful that you will, with me, "rise up and call John blessed."

Steve Brown
Key Life Network

Preface

At one time, it was extremely difficult to find books and resources on the topic of Christian men struggling with lust, pornography, and sexual addictions. These were all taboo subjects. Historically, it's been easy to ignore the fact that many of God's people are struggling deeply, sexually speaking. Often they are a sexual "mess." Sadly, for too many of us, especially our church leaders, the "I'm-okay-you're-okay/don't ask, don't tell" mentality runs deep.

As for the shame-producing and crippling reality of Christian men struggling with same-sex attractions and homosexual pornography—well, forget it. I remember walking into a Christian bookstore years ago and asking the clerk whether they carried a new book on helping Christians struggling with same-sex attractions. The clerk looked at me with a grimace and said, "Well, I should hope not!" Even those who might be seeking a biblical solution to this dilemma were shamed and ostracized, it seems.

Things are different today. A multitude of books, teaching DVDs, and other resources on sexual abuse, pornography, homosexuality, and sexual addictions are now available. That's a good thing! But, many of these resources are technical in nature. Some offer simplistic answers and unrealistic solutions. Some give lots of advice and ten steps to "work" or a host of things to do. I felt led to write a different kind of book.

This material comes from workshops I've presented to men's groups for several years. When I spoke at one church in New York City, scores of men had to be turned away due to lack of space. At another church in the South, I presented a similar workshop at a men's breakfast. The pastor told me to bring about twenty teaching outlines to hand out. He said, "That's about all we get out to these things on a Saturday morning." He was shocked when over one hundred men showed up. It's evident, isn't it? This is where many of our men, youth, and, increasingly, women struggle today. Is it any wonder that many have lost hope that anything will ever change in this life?

Dealing with this problem is much more complicated than following ten steps or learning formulas that ensure success. It requires facing and understanding what's going on in the heart. I wanted to write about what happens to the heart when we neglect soul-care in these crucial areas. What do ongoing, unaddressed struggles with sexual temptation, pornography, and lust do to us relationally and spiritually? Why are we willing to go for years living in the dark prisons we forge for ourselves? What keeps us from walking in the light? How does Jesus meet us in the midst of it to enable us to live changed lives—now? What is the role of the body of Christ, the church, in all of this? Addressing these key questions is my passion in this book.

You need to know that this is not the last word on pornography and lust. It is simply my take on the topic, based on my experience and my understanding of the Scriptures. It's my desire that you as a reader will see God's amazing love for you and for other trapped people—and be led to Christ in a new way, as the One who rescues and redeems. I also hope it speaks to church leadership about the crucial need to stop pretending. Most of us—well, we're all messes, sexually speaking. The sooner we realize that, the sooner we will, in mercy, offer the hope of the gospel in clear and observable ways to those around us who are silently withering away.

I believe there is real hope and help for sexual strugglers. I've been in a mentoring and discipleship ministry with churched sexual strugglers for thirty years. I want to tell you about what happens when God breaks through in hearts that have been deadened by years of pursuing false idols and false intimacy—what happens when men begin to come alive emotionally and relationally, biblically speaking. The gospel is all about seeing what happens when you quit hiding and start to discover the love of the Savior for you—*in* the mess!

So, who is this book written for? It's written for men who know they are dying on the vine internally, spiritually, and relationally, but can't seem to do anything about it. It's for men who are paralyzed with fear and stuck in isolation and secrecy. It's for men who have given up hope and are ready to throw in the towel. It's also for pastors and leaders who have been remiss in pastorally addressing these issues in men's lives. I want them to be better equipped to fearlessly approach these matters. Thus it is also a great tool for leaders and pastors to give to men in their church (for those who admit they struggle and for those who have not yet acknowledged it). Finally, this book is for any struggler who needs to be reminded that the gospel is much bigger than we are—and that God is always calling broken, fallen people to himself to start again.

John Freeman
President
Harvest USA

P. S. Please note that I often use illustrations and examples from ministry situations, but I am careful to change locations, details, and names to protect identities.

Acknowledgments

Over the last several years, I've had many opportunities to speak at men's breakfasts or workshops giving a talk I call, "Keep Yourselves from Idols: Living as Men of Integrity in a Sex-Saturated World." Increasingly, more and more men have come up to me and asked, "Does this material exist anywhere in print form?" After telling them that it doesn't too many times, I took the question as encouragement to begin putting my thoughts about this subject into print. This book is an expanded version of the original talk.

This venture would not have been possible without many collaborators and cheerleaders who offered their time, expertise, and skill to get it completed. Of course, I am so indebted to the New Growth Press team, especially Barbara Juliani and Cheryl White. My editor, Sue Lutz, also believed in this project and was such a great encouragement to me. What a delight and honor to work with each of you!

Nicholas Black, our Education and Resources Director at Harvest USA, took what was really a very rough draft and offered his skill and heart, spending many hours helping me to shape the message I wanted to convey. I couldn't have done this without him and his careful eye. Thank you so much, Nicholas.

I also wish to thank my ministry colleagues at Harvest USA. Much of this content is the result of working with each of you as part of our team, as we challenge and sharpen one another towards gospel clarity in all we do.

Finally, I wish to thank my wife, Penny, who has been beside me over thirty years in ministry. You are, and have been, my principal cheerleader. You often express much more confidence in me than I have in myself. Thank you for believing in me and what Christ is up to in me.

John Freeman

Chapter 1

No One Escapes
Our Sexualized, Pornified
Culture and Its Consequences

I recently had to ask my husband of twenty years to leave our home due to an unrepented and therefore undealt-with pornography problem. Our twenty-year-old son called us this week from another state to tell us he's gay. Our sixteen-year-old daughter has been in counseling for some time now for cutting and self-mutilation, after frequenting some very explicit cyber-sex sites for several years. It had become an overwhelming secret in her life and she just didn't know how to handle the shame, guilt, and feelings of being out of control with it. Then, just recently, my brother's wife left him to pursue a lesbian relationship with another woman.

I had just finished preaching at a church in Florida. Afterwards, as I was shaking hands at the door of the sanctuary, I felt a tap on my shoulder. A lady, probably just a few years younger than I, asked, "Mr. Freeman, can we talk for a moment?" I walked her over to a corner of the sanctuary so we could speak privately. She then related to me the situation summarized above. I was stunned by her candor. It was the utter frankness of her last statement, however, that rendered me almost speechless. She said, "Sexual sin and brokenness of one type or another has impacted every significant relationship in my life."

LIFE IN THE TWENTY-FIRST CENTURY

Welcome to life in the twenty-first century. Or more bluntly, welcome to the increasing "norm" of life in our churches! This is the reality of our over-sexualized, no-holds-barred culture today. The combination of our own fallen hearts and a world that wants us to embrace its fallenness—along with the Evil One who is working behind the scenes in all of this—is what pushes us into the sexual chaos that is now a part of everyday life, even for believers.

Have you ever noticed how hard it is to strive for sexual holiness these days? It's almost impossible. In today's sex-saturated culture, sex sells! It sells products and services, but, even more damaging, it sells our hearts a bill of goods contrary to God's design for us. This is extremely toxic for the soul. Movies, television, music, and advertising discovered the power of sex to sell their products long ago. The result? Everywhere we turn, we're bombarded by hundreds of sexually seductive images many times a day.

The billboard said it all. A beautiful woman peered at me seductively as I passed by, and printed above her photograph were the bold words, "Satisfy Lust." I couldn't tell you what product she was supposed to be selling, but advertisers know that our hearts can be enticed in seemingly countless ways. Maybe it's the abundance of softcore porn magazines at the supermarket, located at eye level above the candy and newspapers, their covers designed to spark the desire of those who struggle with lust. Similar kiosks are on almost every corner of any large city, at the train station or airport. You can't avoid them. But these traps for the heart can appear in seemingly innocent

2

locations as well. I once picked up a map/brochure at my local mall as I looked for the location of a particular store. There on the cover, in full color, was an extremely attractive woman smiling at me over her shoulder. Her back was bare down to the curve of her waist, her lips perched in a suggestive smile. She was twisting a string of pearls around her neck seductively. I immediately thought, *What does this have to do with finding the cell phone store?* Sadly, for men struggling with pornography or sexual addiction, that image alone could start a process that could spiral down into sexual sin later on. It's called a "trigger." And wherever we turn, this kind of imagery is built into the very fabric of life today.

Most of us now know the dangers of computers. Strike the wrong key or enter a word or phrase by mistake and you get something you didn't ask for. My wife learned this the hard way several years ago when she took our twin girls, then eight years old, to see the Broadway play *Annie* when it came to town. The girls wanted to buy Annie sweatshirts at the theater. My wife knew she could probably get a better deal by shopping online, so she innocently typed in something like "Little Orphan Annie," thinking she would get a list of products and stores selling the merchandise. She immediately got a product alright—a disturbing sexual image she hadn't asked for.

I know she is not alone in this experience. It is easy to type in the wrong web address and wind up on the front page of a pornographic site, or put in a search term and see dozens of pornographic sites listed as part of your search results. This is why every household should have some kind of porn filter or accountability software on their computers and mobile devices. At times I'm still amazed at the pushback I get from men who are reluctant to install a filter or accountability software on their computer. For men, youth, and even women who struggle with pornography and lust, that laptop, tablet, or cell phone is like carrying around an adult bookstore all day long. You have to make a decision, sometimes several times a day, as to whether to go into that "bookstore" or not. Sometimes it's all too much for one person to handle alone. I'll talk more about that later in the book.

Do you see how easy it is today to get caught up in this "web"? Everywhere we turn, we encounter opportunities to pursue illicit sexual things. We often don't even have look for it. To borrow biblical language, "sin is crouching at the door" and "its desire is for you"; in other words, to scar your heart sexually (Genesis 4:7).

IS SEXUAL INTEGRITY POSSIBLE WHEN YOU'RE BOMBARDED BY LIES?

How do we consider God's call to holiness in light of what we have to face these days? And don't be mistaken, holiness *is* a crucial issue. Hebrews 12:14 tells us, "Strive for . . . the holiness without which no one will see the Lord." Likewise, James tells us to "keep oneself unstained from the world" (James 1:27). I think every Christian would affirm the difficulty of keeping oneself holy and unstained, given what assaults our souls daily. The world, the Evil One, and our own sinful hearts continually tell us lies. What do those lies sound like? Most of the guys I've ministered to report being bombarded with all kinds of lies. "A little porn won't hurt anyone." "No one will ever know." "It's been a hard day; you deserve a mood-booster." "Your wife doesn't understand your need for sex." "You just have a higher sex drive than other men." "Everyone struggles with this stuff." "You can always repent later." Have you fallen for any of these excuses and rationalizations? Perhaps they're among those little "voices" you hear daily.

The truth is, the Evil One tailor-makes our temptations, speaking lies into the secret places where we struggle most intensely. Trying to walk the road of obedience and holiness today, sexually speaking, isn't for the faint-hearted. For most men I know, the idea of walking in truth, honesty, and freedom from the power of lust and the accompanying misuse of sex, is a pie-in-the-sky, wishful-thinking notion they've given up attaining in this life. I'm increasingly amazed at the resignation regarding persistent sexual sin that I find in many men in our churches today. And, what's worse, when our leaders have this mentality, it's a real tragedy. That resignation to powerlessness is often due to hopelessness that has set in, an attitude of unbelief and despair that reflects hundreds of broken vows to God to never give in again. And the reality of our unbelief that God could actually break into our hearts and defeat these temptations and sin patterns is heartbreaking in a struggler. It's so sad when men, both young and old, feel this way. What's even more heartbreaking is when a church leader feels this way about his own sexual sin.

PAYING ATTENTION TO THE HEART

There is a plague raging in our hearts, our families, and our churches. It's a plague that demands acute care and heart-monitoring. One of my favorite authors, the noted Bible teacher J. C. Ryle, once wrote of the devastating impact of inattention to one's own heart:

> Let me counsel every true servant of Christ to examine his own heart frequently and carefully as to his state before God. This is a practice which is useful at all times: it is specially desirable at the present day. When the great plague of London was at its height, people remarked [noticed] the least symptoms that appeared on their bodies in a way that they never remarked them before. A spot here, or a spot there, which in time of health men thought nothing of, received close attention when the plague was decimating families, and striking down one after another! So ought it be with ourselves, in the times in which we live. We ought to watch our hearts with double watchfulness. We ought to give more time to meditation, self-examination, and reflection. It is a hurrying, bustling age; if we would be kept from falling, we must make time for being frequently alone with God.[1]

It might surprise you to know that Ryle was writing in 1881. Even then, he was calling for close heart examination and care. Now, apply his warning and challenge to the epidemic of sexual temptations and sin today—things that you may be dealing with. Continued neglect here will only lead to more loss of spiritual health. We have to understand that, in our porn-is-the-norm culture, few escape the devastation of the lust and pornography trap. Christians are not exempt. We've got to realize that whatever is impacting the culture out there is also impacting those in the pews—especially our teens. We don't like to admit it. After all, we're Christians and Christians aren't supposed to struggle with those things. Really? The Bible tells us otherwise.

If we were to remove from the Bible all the passages that speak of God's people dealing with sexual sin, especially in the New Testament epistles, then we'd be cutting out a significant portion of Scripture. Let's face it: even though God's people are called to live holy and blameless lives, the Scriptures presuppose that the conflict with the flesh and its accumulated desires and habits will be a major issue for us, even many years after conversion. Does that sound defeatist? I hope not. It's realistic. While the desire for obedience may be a new desire and often an automatic response, especially among new believers, many of us have to *learn* how to say "no" to ungodliness and worldly passions. We're told that it's the work of the Spirit to "train" us to say no to accumulated X-rated desires (Titus 2:12).

SEX IS A GOOD GIFT

Part of the power of sex is that it is something God delights in having his creatures enjoy. Sex was God's idea. I can't think of any other major world religion where God's first recorded words to man and woman were, "Have sex and lots of it!" (Genesis 1:28). (Actually, that's my paraphrase, but look it up—it's true.) I once started a talk to university students with this truth and someone later said to me, "You know, that's sounds like a God worth getting to know." You bet!

But because of the fallen nature of things, we now take a gift like sex, which God meant for good and for blessing, and we turn it into something destructive. Something that was meant to reflect God's love as part of our life, in the right context, comes to dominate our lives and hearts. Teacher and author Paul David Tripp talks about this: "If you allow your heart to be ruled by sex or sexual pleasure or sexual power or whatever other things sex gets you, you will not only misuse this good gift of God but also end up being controlled by it. Sexual distortion and sexual addiction do not exist because sex itself is bad but because we have put it in a place that God never intended it to be. . . . My sex life will be shaped and directed by whatever is my street-level master. And I will only ever stay inside God's wise boundaries when he is the functional ruler of my heart."[2]

Just what or who is our street-level master? It's that thing we give our allegiance to, that thing we bow and submit to. The truth is, when we become followers of Jesus Christ, intent on submitting our lives to him, ready to call him "boss," we can expect struggle. We can expect World War III to break out in our hearts and lives. This is especially true in areas where we've looked to someone or something else besides Christ to bring us a sense of life. We often remain vulnerable to these things even after becoming a Christian. However, that's not really the main dilemma.

Our problem is that we walk in unbelief. We fail to believe that God cares or that he desires to enter into our struggles with the sins of lust, pornography, and sexual temptation. After all, our history of failure is proof that this is just our cross to bear in life. For many men, "white-knuckling it" and enduring it until heaven is the strategy they've come to accept. Is this the attitude you've adopted about your struggles with sin?

Companies today are spending tens of millions of dollars on technology that enables one to sit at a baseball game and watch a porn movie on the cell phone tucked under one's sleeve. Do you think they care whether the user is a Christian or not? It's time for Christians to be honest about how pornography impacts everyone and how we all too often live failure-filled, shame-filled, and guilt-ridden lives. Reticent to admit our sexual temptations and struggles, we hope they will somehow just all go away. But wishing away or ignoring your struggles never works; it just leads to more delusion and faulty thinking. Chapter 5 discusses why we're often so reluctant to be honest about these aspects of our hearts.

Just how prevalent is this war in hearts and lives? Consider these staggering statistics regarding pornography usage.

A SOBERING LOOK AT THE PROBLEM

- "In 2000, as many as 25 million Americans spent 1 to 10 hours per week viewing Internet pornography, and as many as 4.7 million spent over 11 hours per week viewing Internet pornography."[3]
- Pornography usage and online behavior is now a significant factor in two out of three divorces.[4]
- One survey said that as many as 50% of Christian men and 20% of Christian women are addicted to pornography.[5]
- More than 25% of men admit to accessing porn at work, risking their careers and livelihood.[6]
- One out of three visitors to adult websites is a woman.[7]
- Romance novels increasingly contain porn in this $1.4 billion-a-year industry. Romance novels account for 55% of all popular mass-market fiction sold, and psychologists are increasingly concerned that romance novels are emotionally and sexually distorting the way women view relationships.[8]
- 54% of pastors admit to viewing pornography at least a few times in the previous twelve months; 18% admit to visiting explicit websites "between a couple of times a month and more than once a week."[9]

- In a *Christianity Today* Leadership Survey, almost 60% of pastors said pornography addiction is the most damaging issue in their church.[10]
- Among children between the ages of 8 and 16, 90% have viewed pornography on the Internet.[11]
- 80% of 15- to 17-year-olds have viewed hard-core pornography multiple times.[12]
- The average age of first exposure to Internet porn is 11 years old.[13]
- In the U. S., mobile phones are now the preferred way to access pornography, making porn usage and addiction more likely because of its increased accessibility and anonymity.[14]

You'll note that some of these statistics are over ten years old. Nonetheless, this is the most recent data available because Internet pornography statistics become outdated very quickly. Today, I believe you could safely add an increase of at least ten to fifteen percent to any of these statistics. I could have listed another twenty similar statistics, but you probably get the picture. For the most part, pornography statistics are no longer really necessary to convince people of the size and extent of the problem. It's that widespread an epidemic! This sad reality was confirmed by an article I read recently, which talked about a porn research study that had to be scrapped because the researchers could find no control group of young men that had not looked at porn.[15]

Against this backdrop, it's unbelievable that many pastors and church leaders are still reticent to initiate discussions about sex and sexuality in their congregations. In some cases, the willingness to address these struggles as a church is nonexistent. Our efforts to help our people don't come close to the depth of struggle and its impact among our people, which means that something is terribly awry.[16]

I remember speaking to the intercessory prayer team at a church in the Philadelphia area. These good-hearted people had met regularly on a designated weeknight for about six years in order to pray for members of the congregation who requested prayer regarding practical heart concerns. The leaders said something to me that was very telling. "John, over the years we've had people come for prayer about job situations, troubles with children, chaotic issues within the extended family, financial issues, and even marital conflict, but never, ever, has anyone come for prayer regarding sexual struggles or situations."

I was shocked and speechless—well, for a moment or two. I said to them, "That's amazing. I'd be asking myself why not? Why *hasn't* anyone ever come with cries for help and healing?" That church had a problem that is common to ninety-five percent of churches today. Somehow they had been very successful at communicating, intentionally or unintentionally, that they weren't really equipped to deal with sexual sin. So many churches communicate, whether by word or deed, "We're fragile here and we can't handle *that*." I went on to explain that most churches don't give messages that encourage people to talk about these matters, nor do they offer practical, redemptive hope to those whose hearts are in trouble sexually.

Sadly, parents often put their heads in the sand as well, thinking, *Surely not my child!* Yet I can't tell you how many times parents have called me, shocked to discover a child looking at porn. As they begin to investigate, they usually find it's happened multiple times, maybe for several years. Routinely, however, parents resist having an Internet filter on the computer because of their naiveté. In actuality, many young people begin to develop addictive habits by the time they're ten years old. The amazing paradox is that parents fight against shielding their kids from learning how to deal with this and think about it biblically!

A few months ago, I was asked to preach in a church. The topic was "The Gospel in a Sexually Broken World." As I sat next to the pastor, within just a minute or so of getting up to preach, he leaned over to me and said, "You might have noticed that about one-third of the sanctuary is empty today." I had. He then explained, "I received lots of calls and e-mails from concerned parents telling me they weren't coming today. They didn't want their kids hearing about this." Something is dreadfully wrong here.

But that wasn't the only time I've run into this. Harvest USA, the organization I work for, has had several scheduled assembly talks and other opportunities to speak to groups of students cancelled suddenly, too. How sad, especially when statistics show that most parents do not talk about sex or sexual issues with their children at all. (That's another talk I do for parents: "Why you won't or can't talk about sex with your kids.") What a catastrophe for our vulnerable kids! Unfortunately, there are hundreds of other voices out there who will fill in the void created by the silence of their parents! A television commercial I saw recently says it all. A mom was entering her teenage daughter's room. The daughter, who looked around sixteen, was lying on the bed looking at her laptop. The mom, bringing in a basket of folded clothes, stood at the edge of the bed and said, "Oh, I really want to talk to you about your use of the Internet—but that might lead to a conversation about sex, and I'm not ready for that yet." At sixteen! Something's surely amiss!

For men, how do years of inattention impact our besetting sexual temptations and sins? It isn't pretty. It disfigures the image of God in us. It can even alter our psyche and distort our character. Unless God intervenes and we are exposed or until we come to our senses, we can live for many years in three distinct, heart-damaging façades that we will explore in this book.

I first realized this several years ago when our ministry began to develop a strategic plan to improve our services to those who come to us for help. Now, you need to know that words like "strategic plan" cause people like me—random, abstract thinkers—to quake in their boots. It's just so opposite to how my brain operates. But at one point I had to set aside half a day to think about how people have characteristically come into our ministry over the last thirty years—people, primarily men, who have roamed the sexual wilderness alone, hoping that it would someday, somehow, work itself out. Three categories came to mind almost immediately regarding the men who have come into our ministry. Most often, they've become *God-haters, idol-makers*, and *game-players*. In the next several chapters, I'll show how this can happen even to believers, and what these different personas look like.

HOPE FOR THE HOPELESS

But first, are you feeling hopeless? Let me encourage you: This is just the kind of stuff Jesus loves to deal with in our lives. And you aren't alone. Paul reminds the Christians in Corinth, "No temptation has overtaken you that is not common to man" (1 Corinthians 10:13). None of what holds our hearts in bondage is new. While many people decry the state of our culture today, these are actually the very same problems that have been around since man was created. Sex run amok is part of the fall and our brokenness. It always has been. But take heart: neither is it new to the Lord!

Do you not feel, at some level, the impact in your life from all the years of hiding, pretense, and soul-neglect? How it powerfully tempts you to give up? Hang on. God wants to do a new work in your life, but it begins by seeing, much like the Prodigal Son, the pit you've gotten yourself into, how you got there, and what it's done to your heart. That's when you'll see and appreciate what God can do even more! So if you're a struggler (and few among us today aren't), be encouraged.

FOR REFLECTION AND DISCUSSION

1. How does it affect you (intellectually and emotionally) to learn that the Scriptures treat the brokenness of sex as being a routine part of the fallen nature of life for everyone, including

believers? Does that help you deal with your own sexual struggles? Yes/no?

2. Name the ways you have been inattentive and neglectful of your sexual struggles. Where have the temptations you face been most persistent, and where have you been most neglectful?

3. Given the difficulty and challenge of maintaining sexual integrity today, what kind of lies does the Evil One speak into your heart about all this? Where are the places, right now, you're most likely to believe his lies?

Chapter 2

Life as a God-Hater

I was one of the "hidden people" you talked about in your article, John. A child of the damned, one of the children of a lesser God, less than human. I would sit in church, year after year, wondering why I was even there. I taught Sunday school for years, ran clubs at church, was very involved in the men's groups and in every way—all hoping that my works would set me free. For over forty years I continued like this, praying for relief from my sexual temptations and struggles. But no answer. God seemed to answer and work in other areas of my life, but not this one. Nothing.

I received this e-mail from a man who had read about our ministry in an interview in the Christian magazine, *ByFaith*. His words just broke my heart. In that article, I had quoted one of my seminary missions professors, Harvie Conn, who said in 1983 that the gay community was one of the largest "unreached people" groups in America. In the same breath, he stated that the real "hidden people" in our churches today were followers of Christ who had brought all the baggage of their unresolved struggles with pornography, same-sex attractions, sexual abuse, and other life-scarring experiences into their life with Christ—as they sat in our pews. Conn explained that the church usually operates in a "we don't talk about those things around here" mode, which keeps people isolated. When people don't directly, naturally, and on their own see the link between the gospel, their past scars, and their current struggles, they end up spiritually crippled and hopeless—perpetually "hidden"—to the ongoing detriment of their souls and the body of Christ.

In chapter 1, I talked about the fact that Christians are not exempt from any of these struggles. Families today are impacted on multiple levels by sex gone awry. Most men struggle on some level with our broken sexuality and are tempted to misuse sex. We may like to think we're not impacted by our sex-gone-wrong culture, but we are only fooling ourselves. We want to think our temptations and occasional moral failures, whether in our hearts or with our bodies, are not that bad. We like to pretend we're okay. We tend to let things slide, hoping it will all get better on its own. But, let me suggest that inaction is action! Doing nothing about my ongoing sexual temptations and struggles with lust *is* a strategy—one of denial. When it comes to a deep struggle with lust, the results can be devastating. But what is lust actually?

Author and teacher Dr. Dan Allender has something interesting to say about the issue and power of lust. He writes:

> The word can be used to describe a legitimate, godly desire. . . . Strong, passionate, eager desire or lust is not inconsistent with God's purpose for our lives. On the other hand we know from the Bible and from experience that strong desire, or lust, can be immoral and destructive. . . . Destructive lust is any consuming desire that is either out of bounds or out of balance. An out-of-bounds lust is a desire for any person or object or idea that is inconsistent with God's expressed desire for our life. An

out-of-balance lust is any legitimate desire that blocks our ability to serve God and others.[17]

In other words, we can desire someone or something that is expressly prohibited by God (e.g., sexual encounters not with your spouse) and is therefore out of bounds. Or we can allow even legitimate desires to grow so much that we sin against God and another person (e.g., lashing out in anger at a spouse who doesn't want to have sex when you do), which puts that desire out of balance. We often don't realize the power of our lusts, especially if they are the out-of-bounds or out-of-balance kind Allender describes. Left to ourselves, we're often the last ones who can tell when we're in their grip, until it's too late.

LUST AS HEART-HUNGER

Years ago, I developed my own definition of lust. This definition is based on the lust or inordinate desire that takes advantage of another person sexually, even though it may all just be in my thoughts. Most men don't understand how lust captures their hearts. Therefore, a working definition of lust might be this: Lust is that heart-hunger in me that denies and disavows those made in the image of God, whether it's another man or another woman, and reduces them to what I can get out of them to feed (and fill) my hungry heart right now. This means that by nature, our lusts twist, devour, consume, and use others for our own benefit. This is true whether we're viewing a computer screen or watching an illicit DVD, whether we are in real time, in cyber time, in a chat room—or just in our hearts and heads in our own fantasies.

When I describe lust like this, the men who come into our ministry can immediately understand what I'm talking about. Their heart cry is often, "Yes, that's me. I don't want to be like that. But I don't know how *not* to be like that!" In my definition of lust, there's obviously an urge to "meet the needs of my sinful heart right now." There's an intrusive immediacy to lust that often denies the long-term consequences and seeks burning satisfaction or gratification in the moment. We can be in over our heads before we know it. Sex and our use or misuse of it is a powerful force, much bigger than we are.

I like to compare our naïve understanding of sex and our propensity to misuse it to a scene in the original *Jurassic Park* movie. The dinosaurs are on a rampage, destroying everything in their path. The more macho men are out trying to corral or shoot them. The old, white-haired professor is sitting in a gazebo in the theme park with his two grandchildren and a woman scientist. They're eating melting ice cream from the concession stand since the electricity has failed. With a faraway look in his eye, the old professor starts to talk about the situation. "The next time I try these experiments, I think I'll . . ." The woman scientist stops him mid-sentence and counters his blasé attitude with something like, "What do you mean 'the next time'? Don't you know you've let out a power much bigger than you are and it won't ever go back to normal?" She's bringing home the point that he had unleashed something too large to control, a devastating force that kills and takes no captives. This is the way it is with our untamed sexual passions and lusts. Once they're out, they will continue to wreak havoc for years and years unless we seek to know what's going on (that is, the non-sexual heart issues behind them), in order to understand how the gospel must meet us in that very moment, and have a plan to corral them.

A LOVE/HATE, SLOW-BOIL RELATIONSHIP WITH GOD

When these things control our hearts and lives over the course of years, they will first make you a *God-hater*. This is a very destructive characteristic I've seen in the men who've come into our ministry. When I've confronted them with this, many of those men have responded, "What? How is that even possible? I love Jesus, you know." You may be saying the same thing. I don't doubt that you may love Jesus and be committed to walking with him. It has been my experience, however, that when men have developed a pornified heart and experienced the up-and-down, success–failure–success–failure cycle of this struggle, there is always something going on underneath! There is often a love/hate, slow-boil relationship going on with God, a cynicism that dares God to ever do anything redemptive about it all.

This is true especially when our hearts regularly reject some of God's attributes, simply wishing that they weren't there. For example, we deny the unavoidable fact that God knows all and sees all. We don't want to acknowledge that he sees not only what we do, but also what we think and desire in our hearts—things no one else knows. This is one area of life where knowing that God knows, sees, and is intimately acquainted with all your ways isn't a very comforting thought. It actually can cause us a lot of distress.

The reason I know this love/hate thing goes on between men and God is because I've experienced it not just in my own inner struggles but also in my marriage. I've been married for thirty-five years now, and the intimacy and love I've experienced in my marriage is indescribable. There's nothing quite like the comfort and security that comes when someone knows you so truly and sees you so clearly. You're on the same page in so many ways. You may have experienced it, too. You're in a crowded room, maybe twenty feet apart. Something happens, or someone (perhaps a speaker) says something, and your eyes immediately meet those of your wife and you know you're both thinking the same thing. Or maybe you start to ask her for something or start a sentence, and your wife anticipates what you need or finishes the sentence for you. I love that. I love being known like that—most of the time. If I am honest, there are times when I don't like it at all!

I definitely don't like being known when I've been caught. That is, I don't like it when I'm seen and known for who I really am, in my fallen heart and with my sin. I don't like being seen or known when

I respond inappropriately, impatiently, insensitively, or when I really blow it. I don't like it when I put my foot in my mouth and she shoots me one of those "I can't believe you said that" looks. At those times, I don't like being known at all. I don't like that kind of intimacy. In fact, I hate it. And being known at those times often results in a disdain and contempt—for *her*! At those times I'd just rather slink away and disappear. When my foolishness is exposed, I just want to vanish into thin air. I want to run from the fact that someone knows me that well and sees me as I really am.

It's the same way with God. Take the experience you've had of others knowing your personal record of failures, of feeling caught and desiring to shrink away from the other person's presence. Now, multiply it by 100 with God. As the writer to the Hebrews says, "no creature is hidden from his sight, but all are naked and exposed to the eyes of him to whom we must give account" (Hebrews 4:13). Given many of our sexual histories, how could this just-wanting-to-disappear, love/hate relationship with God *not* be the basic way we relate to him?

When you've wrestled for years in your cycles of success and defeat with sexual sin, even, or especially, as a believer, it does something to you that's not pretty. You've experienced years of unrelenting emotional and spiritual temptations and failures and, perhaps, debilitating waves of hopelessness over it all. You've made thousands of vows of "Never again." You've turned over every "new leaf" you can think of. How many times have you made a New Year's resolution that *this* is the year you'll conquer it all and turn it over to the Lord, once and for all? If this is your experience, how could there *not* be a slow-boil anger always percolating under the surface about it all—and how could that anger not be directed at God?

I've been in ministry in this area long enough to say that I've never known a man who wrestled unproductively with lust and sexual sin who *doesn't* have a deep anger problem. And my experience has also shown that the flip side is just as true—I've never met a man who had a deep-seated anger problem who did not have secret sexual sin abounding. How is this anger revealed and how does it relate to ongoing sexual struggles?

Our anger usually manifests itself in our lives in one of three directions. First, this beneath-the-surface anger is often turned toward others. In a man who struggles deeply with no resolution in sight, it often turns into an abusive way of relating to the people around him, especially those closest to him. He can be the man who knows his theology well but often hides behind it. He is also more than likely overbearing, gruff, and unloving to those in his life. He can become the man who demands perfection in all things with everyone he knows. On the home front, he's the husband and father who runs a tight ship, with little time for the failures or imperfections of others. He's someone for whom, more than likely, the wife and children have to prepare, mentally and emotionally, for his daily 6:00 p.m. homecoming. He's often the person whose anger is out in the open, and no one can win an argument with him; or his anger is stuffed inward, and the resulting coldness and silence he displays can shut down any attempt at discussion.

In the early days of my marriage, as I was trying to work out my own history of sexual brokenness and its residue, my wife often called me the "prosecuting attorney." I had to win every argument. I had to have the last word with no loose ends. I had to appear competent and in control of all things—because my inner life was often in such turmoil. Interestingly, seminary only exacerbated this, because I felt under even more pressure to look good and do everything right. So, while my inner life was out of control, I insisted that people march to my drumbeat. Since I couldn't manage my inner life, I did everything I could to manage everyone and everything "out there."

A second direction this anger is expressed is inward, directed toward the self. This can take the form of self-destructive behaviors or styles of relating that act as punishment for or insulation from guilt, shame, and loss of hope. By the time most men get into our ministry or begin to work on their issues, they can also be cross-addicted to mood-altering substances like alcohol or prescription drugs. The burden of what they've been dealing with, year after year, and for some men, decades, has become too much. They seek further escape by numbing themselves with various substances, but that only drives them more into their compulsive sexual behavior, which was their original escape from the difficulties of life.

More often than not, these are also the "silent" men in our congregations, those who have abdicated leadership in their marriages and in the home, becoming passive in all things. They cease to interact with their wives and children in a way that is consistently loving and life-giving to them. So, when I see either overly strong and dominant men or men who have dropped out of life, the first thing I think about is where they struggle sexually.

This inner anger and performance-based living can also take the form of a man who is the overconfident overachiever with extremely high performance goals for himself and all those in his life. These men can be quite successful, respected, and admired from afar by others— the kind of man no one can believe is entrapped in sexual sin, even when it is exposed. We say, "No way. Not him!" Sadly, pastors and church leaders often fit this category.

The third direction anger can take is toward God. He hasn't seemed to come through as you'd hoped he would. You've prayed and tried to no avail, like the guy who wrote me that e-mail at the beginning of the chapter. The feeling that God hasn't heard you does something to you. Your prayer life and your relationship with God can become skewed. Prayers for help and change take on a life of their own. They center on the repetitive plea of "God forgive me, forgive me, forgive me, help me, help me, help me," or "God, change me change me, change me."

Now, there's nothing wrong—and something absolutely right—about calling out to God in our desperation and need, asking for his help. But when this kind of prayer becomes the essence of our life and our heart-cry, especially when we see little movement or real change, it can set us up not only for a lot of inner anger, but also bitterness and contempt toward God. This is true of most men who seek help after years of struggle in this area.

HOPE DEFERRED MAKES THE HEART SICK

Think about the man at the beginning of this chapter who labeled himself one of the "hidden people." Reread the shame-filled, debasing language he used to describe himself.

When I initially read that e-mail, my first thought was that this guy couldn't possibly be a believer. But then I realized two things. First, he had been reading my denomination's magazine. Second, he talked about his years of prayer and involvement in his church. It hit me: Here was a man proving the truth of Proverbs 13:12: "Hope deferred makes the heart sick." Here was a truly disillusioned, heart-sick man, due to his years of struggle during which God did not seem to answer his prayers for deliverance!

I often have men come into my office for an initial interview before getting them involved in one of our support/integrity groups. I want to hear a little of their personal story. I want to try to discern if we can actually help them and if they're a candidate for our ministry; that is, if they're at the place in their lives where they are actually desperate for God to show up and do something new. Many times I've had men volunteer in our first meeting, right off the bat, "I've prayed for years about all this but nothing's happened. God hasn't answered my prayers, so what do you have to say to me now?" Actually, that's a very good question. If I had a dollar for every time it's been asked over the years, I could probably retire to Tahiti. And it's all due to an anger and cynicism that's taken root with and about God.

As we sit with these men and try to unravel just where and how their hearts have "gone south" in all this, I begin to see that, quite often, they have related to God like Aladdin rubbing the genie's lamp. They expect God to grant their requests and, over time, when nothing happens, they become more demanding. When I suggest to them that a much better, more effective prayer would center around knowing God in the midst of their struggle and distress, asking him to give them a heart to love and serve him and others regardless of their pain, they look at me with a blank stare. They don't know what I'm talking about. Why? Because the background noise of their struggles and their long personal history of defeat drowns out everything but their intense desire to quickly and magically get out of their pain. That's certainly understandable. After all, no one is exempt from relating to God like that at times. But in their attempt to escape the pain, disappointment, and lousy state of their hearts, they have actually rejected God without knowing it. That is the root of the sarcasm and anger over God's inaction, and the reason they find themselves in a no-man's-land of very real despair.

What's happened is that the believer has begun to relate to God and pray like a pagan. What do I mean by that? Several years ago, Tim Keller, senior pastor at Redeemer Presbyterian Church in New York City, preached a sermon called "The Basis of Prayer" from a series of sermons based on the Lord's Prayer in Matthew 6. He made the point that, when we lose sight of our status as a child of God, we can begin to pray like religious people, not God's children. Our prayers take on a business-relationship format based on our performance, based on what I'm doing right (or in this case, what I've done wrong) as opposed to a father-child relationship. But, when we approach God in both desperation *and* expectation, that kind of prayer is natural to the father-child relationship.

Men who have struggled for years with no resolution to their sexual temptations and sin have lost that father–son relational pattern that is so critical. They've begun relating in prayer with a business model, hence the "babbling" kind of prayer that Matthew 6:7 talks about. This includes the unrealistic demands of "change me," "stop me," "help me," all of which are devoid of recognizable familial relationship. As a result, we cease to be aware that the process of prayer between our Father God and us, his children, is just as important as the tiny yet significant petition part. In other words, prayer is not a magic incantation to achieve a desired result or the right sequence of buttons on a vending machine that will yield the snack you crave. Prayer is a conversation that allows a Father to help shape the character of his son. If all their conversations only involve the son asking for the same thing over and over again, not only will they never grow closer, the son will never learn what the Father is trying to teach him by not just giving him what he asks.

In a scene from the movie *Shadowlands*, C. S. Lewis's wife, Joy, was experiencing a remission of the cancer that would eventually take her life. In one scene, Lewis is sharing the news with his fellow professors at Cambridge and rejoicing that Joy is now much better. Another professor pipes up and says, "See there, Lewis—your prayers are working, they're changing things." To which Lewis replies, "Oh, I don't pray to change things. Prayer changes me." I don't know whether Lewis actually said that in real life, but this is an excellent point for the sexual struggler. When God doesn't seem to change things—when he doesn't seem to come through by freeing me from my temptations and sin—it has to affect my prayer and life with God in some not-so-good ways. We cease to have an awareness of his presence in our lives and heart struggles, in spite of our pleading prayers. And thus we unwittingly become God-haters. But that's not all. It gets worse.

FOR REFLECTION AND DISCUSSION

1. One writer defined lust as "out-of-bounds" or "out-of-balance." John defined it as a "heart-hunger" that uses other people to fill

your hungry heart. Where do you find yourself in both those definitions? How much does lust consume your mind and attention?

2. Do you see anger as being a characteristic or pattern in your life? Go back and read the way anger is described—as being expressed outward or inward. Can you begin to see the connection between your sexual struggles and anger? Are you willing to ask someone who knows you well to speak into this issue with you?

3. Can you think of times when God seemed absent and far-removed in your struggle against sin? What does that feel like? Do you find your prayer life empty and frustrating?

Chapter 3

Life as an Idol-Maker

Derek was twenty-three years old. A friend had referred him to Harvest USA and he launched right into his story with me. He had become a Christian in high school and had been very involved in his church's youth group. He told me that he had really started to grow in his knowledge of Christ during those years. He had secretly struggled with pornography for some time, however.

He told me that at the same time he was growing in his relationship with Christ, "the images and lies that porn promised me all began to compete with my walk with God." As he started to follow his desires, he increasingly compromised his own holiness. He began to view Internet porn on a regular basis.

"John, it soon became an addiction," he said, and it had gone downhill ever since. With every passing year, he found himself drowning in his secret sin, crossing boundaries he never thought he would cross. He lived in depression and knew that giving in to these things had taken a devastating toll on his identity and all his relationships.

He often felt sorrowful because of the way his straying had broken fellowship with God and other people. He admitted that he now isolated himself because of where his desires had led him. "John, I rage against all sound judgment, even as I still feel God, from time to time, convicting my heart." He was sinking deeper now, sometimes several times a day, not just into pornography, but into sexually explicit chat rooms and cyber-sex. It had crossed over from a private thing, involving just him, to involving other people, albeit anonymously.

"God has already taken away the lampstand from my life," he told me. "I am no longer a credible witness. I am narcissistic, proud, and self-righteous. The times I've been faithful to God are becoming more of a distant memory." And all this had happened by the time he was twenty-three! He went on to say that, deep down inside, he wanted freedom from it all. "I want to regain the essence of who I once was and who I know God wants me to be now. But I see no way out. Help! Please. I know I need God and others. Is there any way out of this pit?"

Do you feel the absolute desperation of this young man's life? Did you hear the frenzied tone of his story, the despair that comes when you exhaust all your human resources? Impersonal statistics may convey the scope and depth of the problems "out there," but a story like this makes us understand something that those statistics can never convey. It shows us the human picture of what sliding into the gorge and falling over the cliff look like, spiritually and sexually speaking.

Second, this story demonstrates that no one sets out to get addicted to sin. Rather, we get hooked on, addicted to, and oriented toward the things to which we give our hearts on an ongoing basis. We start to become like the things we go to for life, and over time our life becomes chaotic and disordered, and we find ourselves as powerless and dead as the idols we look to. My friend's story is a step-by-step view into the life of someone who once had a vital, thriving walk with God but who no longer enjoys any kind of walk with him at all. The life he once had is no longer visible. It shows that without living in the gospel, we're doomed. Can you identify? Maybe that's where you are right now.

This story shows us that our hearts naturally cling to and worship the things that falsely offer life, the things that promise a taste of euphoria in our otherwise bland existence. Pornography offers a sensual and sensory detonation, which science tells us can—if indulged in frequently and long enough—rewire the brain itself. Little wonder that, for many men, our compulsions or addictions become our illicit playground, the place we escape to, seeking some semblance of emotional "okay-ness." In that sense, it's like a drug.

The temptation to look to other things for life came first to Adam and Eve (Genesis 3:6). They had to decide if they would follow and obey God or if they would seek the "something else" that seemed to promise life. Now, if our first parents fell into unbelief and sin in an environment that had all the peace, security, and provision God could offer, then how much more vulnerable are we to our fallen and warped passions!

Unfortunately, an increasing number of men and boys in our churches resemble Derek, but at even earlier ages. Several months ago I walked into our offices and saw one of our staff, David White, staring off into space at his desk. I asked, "What's up?" He told me that in just a few weeks' time, several parents had brought their middle-school sons into the office, all either deeply hooked on porn or newly proclaiming their "coming out" as gay. Not only was Dave sad that this was their reality so early in life, but he was also impacted by the sober reality that these kids were headed down the road of a lifelong sexual idolatry struggle—unless God intervened in big ways.

IDOL-MAKERS

In our ministry, we've seen over and over again that unless God intervenes in the lives of strugglers and unless they allow Christ into their despair, there will be another devastating consequence in their lives.

A second persona will come to characterize their hearts as men with years of soul-neglect regarding their sexual struggles. They will live life as **idol-makers.**

We build, turn to, and bow to counterfeit idols so easily. The Bible views it as the natural character of the fallen heart. Theologian John Calvin once said, "We may gather that man's nature, so to speak, is a perpetual factory of idols."[18] This is all too true when it comes to sexual sins, especially the use of pornography. I once did a study of what the Bible says about idol worship, particularly the role of "household" idols. One of the surprising things I found was just how much the Bible talks about idolatry—especially in the lives of believers! Even as believers, we are so naturally attracted to idols that in 1 John 5:21, the apostle John admonishes us by saying, "Little children, keep yourselves from idols." While the issue of idolatry is found all over the New Testament, especially in the Epistles, it is spoken of frequently in the Old Testament as well. A study of the kings of Israel reveals that the kings were either tearing down idols or erecting them constantly—sometimes both, if their hearts strayed from God. Sometimes kings started off as good guys but then their hearts "went south" and they turned to idol worship.

With household idols, there was often a more personal, intimate thing going on. In the Old Testament, people sometimes kept small idols of the local deities from other nations in their home just in case the Lord didn't show up! They were a kind of second-tier insurance policy—or so people thought—merchandise that could bless or save them in a crisis. Today, we all too often do the same thing. We hold on to personal idols that, more than likely, aren't a small statue in our house but rather are whatever our hearts turn to or cling to instead of God to bring a sense of well-being to our souls.

What are our household idols today? Well, they can be many things, but they are often sexual in nature. A household idol can be anything we turn to that makes us feel alive in some sense. If we are honest, we have to admit that a counterfeit thing can offer temporary comfort and distraction. Our version of household idols is often our "Plan B" for when God doesn't show up, seems far away or unavailable, or just doesn't seem to be coming through for us. They can be the things we turn to when life is confusing, scary, difficult, or overwhelming—because the payoff is pretty immediate.

In the lives of many men, the household idol of misused sex in its many forms is the surface idol, the thing seen most clearly. But the surface idols (pornography, masturbation, sexual fantasies, chat rooms, cyber-sex, etc.) point to deeper, hidden idols of the heart that many men don't see at all. These deeper idols help to make the sexual behaviors compulsive and addictive. That is, men vainly attempt to stop only the surface idols, but apart from digging down deeper to the hidden idols and uncovering them—understanding their power and control over the heart—the struggler can't break free.

The functional role of an idol feels the same as an addiction or compulsion. We turn to them in an instant, without even being aware of what we are doing. They may even seem foolish to us, but we cling to them because, at some level, we have turned to them for life. When the thing our heart desperately desires is seemingly unattainable, we will grab for something else instead. We'll create a god of our own making, a false god that brings us a sense of security and comfort—a substitute for the real thing. You don't have to go far in the Bible to see the anarchy that results when one turns from the real God to a counterfeit.

As a seminary student, one of the first texts I had to translate from the original Hebrew was chapters 32–34 of the book of Exodus. It's the story of Moses, leaving the people he was leading to the Promised Land to go up on Mount Sinai to meet with God. Now, you must remember that Moses was God's representative to the people. He was the closest thing to God the people could get. In a sense, to be near Moses *was* to be near God. To be in Moses's presence *was* to be in

God's presence. We're even told that when Moses met with God, some of God "rubbed off" onto Moses and the people could see in his face God's reflected glory (Exodus 34:29–35). This resulted in a combination of attraction and fear toward Moses among the people. It was both comforting and terrifying to be near him, which was an accurate picture regarding God, as well. The people were afraid and would not come to Moses until he "called to them . . . and talked with them" (34:31). But to be with Moses was the most intimate the people could be with God. This is important to remember in light of what happens in Exodus 32.

We read in Exodus 32:1, "When the people saw that Moses delayed to come down from the mountain, the people gathered themselves together to Aaron and said to him, 'Up, make us gods who shall go before us. As for this Moses, the man who brought us up out of the land of Egypt, we do not know what has become of him.'" Aaron tragically followed the will of the people. He took their gold items and fashioned them into a golden calf. Then Aaron said, "These are your gods." Then we're told that the people "sat down to eat and drink and rose up to play" (32:6).

That last phrase, "rose up to play," is interesting. Another translation says that the people "sat down to eat and drink and got up to indulge in revelry" (NIV). Another translation defines the "revelry" as Israel "sinning sexually" (NCV). Whenever I read this passage, I picture the scene in the classic film *The Ten Commandments* where the people are wildly jumping up and down, hanging all over each other in a riot of sensuality—at least as much sensuality as the censors would allow in 1956. Today, that scene would probably be much more sexually graphic—and it would come closer to being accurate!

I've gone to some lengths to describe all this for a reason. The book of Exodus provides an amazing example of our natural propensity to turn to counterfeit idols and the way that involves sex. Thus, the essence of Israel's sin at the foot of Mount Sinai might easily and realistically be summed up like this: "Where's Moses?" (Meaning "Where's God?") "I don't know." "Oh, let's make an idol, get drunk, and have an orgy." From "Where's God" to sexual sin? You bet! Do you see it?

THE DEFAULT MODE OF OUR HEARTS

Sadly, nothing has changed about fallen human nature. After God judged the world with the flood, which was supposed to be a new beginning, he said, "The intention of man's heart is evil from his youth" (Genesis 8:21). But, isn't that what God said *before* the flood wiped out almost all human, animal, and plant life? Yes. Genesis 6:5 reads, "every intention of the thoughts of his heart was only evil continually." The default mode of our sinful hearts is always to turn to a counterfeit to replace the real thing. Sexual sin in any form is an attempt to seek after a grander experience, on par with being overwhelmed and awed by the living God. Sexual sin is, at its core, a worship disorder. That's why our search for true spiritual intimacy can get us involved in some pretty extreme, destructive stuff, sexually speaking. G. K. Chesterton is said to have once remarked, "Every man who knocks on the door of a brothel is looking for God." I don't know if he really said that or not, but these words make the point really well! When we go looking for sexual intimacy, we are ultimately seeking intimacy with God. There you have it!

Let's apply what this means. Every man visiting that computer porn site, going to that adult bookstore, frequenting that gentlemen's club, entering that gay bar, hitting that gay bathhouse, or every woman devouring that romance novel (many of which are now hardcore written porn) and visiting porn sites or engaging that stranger in Internet chat-rooms—well, they're all looking for God—in the counterfeit!

That's why, in our ministry, we're always pointing men and women back to the Lord—the real thing versus the counterfeits they've allowed to overshadow God in their lives. The Lord, through his Spirit, puts the desire into the hearts of his people to even *want* to begin to want him, but many caught in the bondage of sin need help to redirect their hearts toward the true and living God. We need both supernatural and peer help to start to believe and keep believing that our God has much more for us than we can imagine. He is the One who promises so much more than the false appeal and distractions of our petty idols.

Part of the fall and the broken nature of things is that our hearts all too easily believe the lies, false promises, and appeal of our idols, especially the sexual idols we've come to depend on. The nature of the false worship I've been talking about in this chapter illustrates the degree of our brokenness. But, what does brokenness look like? How is it tied to our sexual lives? Pastor and author Scotty Smith talks about a brokenness that is different from the feeling we experience when we realize that we have been serving false idols (this is the subjective feeling of repentance that we sometimes experience). Smith talks about an *objective brokenness*, that is, a brokenness that comes from living for the things in life that we make and serve as God-substitutes. This is the brokenness of idolatry. Smith says:

> Something is broken to the degree it doesn't reveal God's glory and serve the purposes of His story.... The main image Scripture uses to demonstrate [such brokenness] is idolatry or false worship—that is, giving anything or anyone the adoration, attention, allegiance, and affection of which Jesus alone is worthy. Paul describes a "broken heart" as one which has "exchanged the truth of God for a lie, and worshiped and served created things rather than the Creator..."[19]

Smith is quoting here from Romans 1, a powerful passage that goes on to reveal all kinds of resulting "idolatries," many of which are of a sexual and sensual nature. When we bow down to the false idols of fantasy, porn, and masturbation, we're truly in the throes of a worship disorder, as some have labeled the theme of this passage. We fall into a pit from which we can't extract ourselves, and we end up living there! Do you ever feel this way—that you're in a pit and there is no way out? And because of that, do you ever feel a deadness in your heart that you wish wasn't so?

Scripture abounds with examples of what idol worship will do to our hearts, even though we're often the last ones to see its deadening effects on us. That's the dark and deceptive nature of sin. In our struggles with temptation and sin, we often take the bait without seeing the hook and, therefore, don't consider how it will rob us of the very life we are looking for. What happens when we "take the bait" of the temporary rush of sexual sin over a long period of time? In Psalm 115:3–8 we read:

> Our God is in the heavens;
> > he does all that he pleases.
> Their idols are silver and gold,
> > the work of human hands.
> They have mouths, but do not speak;
> > eyes, but do not see.
> They have ears, but do not hear;
> > noses, but do not smell.
> They have hands, but do not feel;
> > feet, but do not walk;
> > and they do not make a sound in their throat.
> Those who make them become like them;
> > so do all who trust in them.

Habakkuk 2:18–20 says something very similar:

> "What profit is an idol
> > when its maker has shaped it,
> > a metal image, a teacher of lies?

For its maker trusts in his own creation
   when he makes speechless idols!
Woe to him who says to a wooden thing, Awake;
   to a silent stone, Arise!
Can this teach?
Behold, it is overlaid with gold and silver,
   and there is no breath at all in it.
But the Lord is in his holy temple. . . ."

I want you to think about two things from these passages. First, notice how Psalm 115 begins—and how Habakkuk 2 ends. We're told first that "Our God is in the heavens; he does all that he pleases," and we end with the truth that "The Lord is in his holy temple." These two passages are just saying the same thing in different ways. That's significant! You see, there are only two alternatives. Either we can trust, serve, and worship the living God as he is—the mighty, often unpredictable God who won't be put into any of our human categories or boxes—or we can forge gods or idols of our own making that we can manipulate but in reality are dead things. The choice is always ours. We can worship the real and true God or bow to one that is really lifeless, that has "no breath in it."

A NEW KIND OF LIFE

Even as I write about this idea—that we can either continue in the way we've gone for so many years or risk believing that God has something new and better for us—I think of Steve. He was forty-five when I first met him. A very successful businessman, he ran a series of successful yacht clubs for most of his adult life. However, Steve had struggled with same-sex attraction for most of his life. For over twenty years Steve's life was absorbed by pornography, anonymous sex, and gay relationships, some lasting several years.

But there came a time when God interrupted Steve's life in a very dramatic way, a way that was extremely frightening to him at first. Having begun attending AA meetings to deal with his drinking problem, Steve still frequented gay bars and had several short-term relationships. But as he began to deal with his drinking, he was thrown into a new kind of crisis. He had been medicating his heart to cover all kinds of pain and confusion. I remember him telling me, "I would go to the bars and sit there, looking at all those other lonely guys, but somehow I couldn't relate anymore." Feeling that his whole life was turned upside down, one day Steve just honestly blurted out, "God, this is the only thing I've ever known. What am I going to do now?"

In God's providence, shortly after that Steve found out about one of our Bible study support groups for men dealing with all kinds of sexual messes in their lives. He began to understand and respond to the gospel, making a profession of faith in Christ. Of course, none of his feelings, temptations, or emotional tugs-of-the-heart immediately stopped. He had years of built-up coping mechanisms and core beliefs about life that still ruled his heart. But, in something that can only be described as a new work of God in his life, he began to believe that God was calling him toward a different path as a follower of Jesus. He had to make the choice to follow Christ or continue on as he had lived for years. He admitted to me that leaving the life he had always known was terrifying.

Over the next several years, Steve deepened his fellowship with other men who were learning how to turn away from what they once thought would bring them "life" to turn instead to the living God. Steve reported that he had a new sense of purpose. Something inside had changed. Steve began to develop a personal relationship with Christ and started to apply the gospel to what had fueled his pursuit of sex outside God's boundaries. As he did this, living in the light with other men, he told me that the loneliness and insecurity that had plagued his life (even as a successful businessman) began to be replaced by a new sense of purpose and the ability to see his struggles in a new light. Christ began to be the intimate, personal friend Steve had always been looking for in those dark and destructive places, where sex on his own terms had been the dominant force in his life. When Steve stepped into the unknown, the God he had begun to know and trust now paved the way for a new kind of life.

BROKEN CISTERNS AND STIFF-NECKED PEOPLE

Psalm 115 and Habakkuk 2 aren't the only passages of Scripture, though, that point out to us the alternatives of pursuing the true God or chasing after idols. The prophet Isaiah uses the metaphor of kindling a fire and lighting our own torches rather than walking in God's light (that is, trusting in and relying on him), and Jeremiah talks about forsaking God, who is the fountain of living water, and going after water of their own. Those who decide to live by their own light, and those who drink water that doesn't come from God, are assigned by God to live with, and suffer under, their choices.

Isaiah 50:11 tells us,

> Behold, all you who kindle a fire,
>   who equip yourselves with burning torches!
> Walk by the light of your fire,
>   and by the torches that you have kindled!
> This you have from my hand:
>   you shall lie down in torment.

And that theme is repeated by Jeremiah in 2:11–13:

> "Has a nation changed its gods
>   even though they are no gods?
> But my people have changed their glory
>   for that which does not profit.
> Be appalled, O heavens, at this;
>   be shocked, be utterly desolate,

declares the LORD,
for my people have committed two evils:
they have forsaken me,
  the fountain of living waters,
and hewed out cisterns for themselves,
  broken cisterns that can hold no water."

Do you see what both of them are getting at? When we walk outside God's light and insist on finding life on our own terms (even though in the recesses of our minds we know it won't work out), and when we seek not after God but after an idol and draw from it the water we think will give us life, we will one day pay bitterly for refusing to run to God and find life in him.

The second thing I want you to notice from Psalm 115 and Habakkuk 2 is the way these passages demonstrate how at some point we start to resemble the thing we worship. We begin to look like our idols. Their characteristics rub off on us and threaten to destroy the image of God in us. That's what happened to Derek, the young man I spoke about at the beginning of the chapter. Rarely can a person so out of control see his issues so clearly and describe so succinctly his downward spiral into the sexual abyss. But, this guy "got it." He saw that he had lost the ability to do the right thing anymore. Recognizing the dismal state of his heart, he rightly labeled his actions an "addiction." By doing that, Derek was able to do what others find to be almost impossible. I find that most men tend to minimize the frequency and impact of their secret sins. He did not.

Think about what had happened to him. In just a few short years, Derek went from having a strong relationship with God to barely holding on. He felt increasingly powerless in his life, which mirrors Psalm 115's warning that we will begin to look like our idols. We think they will give us life, but they are lifeless and powerless. The cisterns Derek had dug and the torches he had lit for himself, outside of Christ and over against the things of God, had a devastating impact on his heart, his life, his relationships, and his walk with Christ. He's a vivid example of the warnings from Scripture regarding idolatry. Derek's stunning descent is a sobering reminder to heed what the apostle John said about the futility of pursuing idols, "Little children, keep yourselves from idols (1 John 5:21). But what John said right before that is why pursing idols makes no sense: "And we know that the Son of God has come and has given us understanding, so that we may know him who is true; and we are in him who is true, in his Son, Jesus Christ. *He is the true God and eternal life*" (1 John 5:20, italics added). Here, once more, Scripture contrasts the real and the false, and we're left with a decision about where we'll go for real life.

Perhaps you understand what I'm talking about. Your daily life is one of lighting your own torch and digging your own cistern sexually. You know there is no future in a life like this, but, like Derek, you can't see any way out. You've stopped believing that life can be lived any other way than at the foot of your sexual household gods. You've tried and failed over and over.

Your experience is much like the way God described his people Israel in their journey out of Egypt. God often called them "stiff-necked" people. "Stiff-necked" is a term used to describe an animal that stiffens up and will not allow its owner to put a yoke around its neck. A yoke is a wooden frame used to join together two animals, usually oxen, to pull heavy loads. When put in the yoke, the animals would often refuse to submit, to be handled by their owners. God called his people stiff-necked for refusing his yoke of merciful leadership. They were determined to go their own way and settle for shortcuts. Did you know that God first uses this phrase to describe his people just after their fall into idolatry and sexual anarchy in the golden calf incident? In Exodus 32:9, we read that an infuriated God tells Moses while on Mt. Sinai, "I have seen this people, and behold, it is a stiff-necked people." Their idolatry and the debasement that followed had terrible ramifications. It was the start of a history of idol-making and idol-grabbing that characterized God's people for years to come.

Jesus picks up this image of being stiff-necked and of using a yoke. But in a marvelously impassioned way, he makes it very personal and hopeful. In Matthew 11:28–30, he says, "Come to me, all who labor and are heavy laden, and I will give you rest. Take my yoke upon you and learn from me, for I am gentle and lowly in heart, and you will find rest for your souls. For my yoke is easy and my burden is light."

Men who wrestle deeply with sexual sin, with a history of failure, with scarred and polluted hearts, who know the reality of their miserable record, are men who know intimately the yoke of bondage, but they need to learn to live under a different yoke, and that yoke, Jesus promises, is what will give them rest.

You might be thinking, "The idea of rest and the reality of my struggles—well, they just don't seem to go together. In fact, I'm tired. I'm war-worn. I'm about ready to throw in the towel." If this is how you feel, it is the best possible place for you to be in order for God to work in your life. Maybe God is putting his finger on some of these sexual idols of yours, whatever they may be. Maybe for the first time you can hear him saying, "No more. This isn't for you any longer. It's time to give this up. I have a better plan for you."

Maybe he's speaking to your heart once again, telling you that it's not too late to begin again. That's his nature, isn't it? He will continue to pursue us. He never tires of doing that. Do you believe that? It's true. Don't harden yourself. In your pursuit of the false intimacy that your idols have promised, don't become stiff-necked by minimizing the impact of what you are doing, staying in isolation, or not being honest with anyone else. Instead, yield to his touch, his voice, that conviction which is of the Spirit. It's all of God.

FOR REFLECTION AND DISCUSSION

1. Can you identify with Derek's story of his downward slide into despair and depression? Are there any elements in his story that are similar to yours?

2. When God seems unapproachable, unavailable, or far away, where are you tempted to make your own idols, like the Israelites did, and depend on your own resources to make your life work? Can you name some of the idols you see yourself living for?

3. Psalm 115 speaks of a heart that has become hard, and eventually feels dead, through continual trusting in idols. How do you see this operating in your life? In what ways are you just going through the motions regarding your life with God and other people?

Chapter 4

Life as a Game-Player

Tim was a teacher at a large suburban high school, a man in his mid-forties. He told me that he often got that irritated, unsettled, ill-at-ease feeling late at night, usually around ten o'clock. Maybe you know what I'm talking about. It's a set of feelings that overtake you, putting you in a sort of "spell" or trance where you don't even feel like yourself. For Tim, it would kick in late in the evening. Then, like most addicts, he'd begin his ritual. He'd make some excuse to his wife about needing to "go out" for a while. He knew she would retire early, as usual, and not really know when, or if, he returned home before the wee hours of the morning.

Tim would drive around for a while, maybe an hour. He'd always find himself at one of the few remaining adult bookstores in the city and pull into the parking lot, often parking just out of view of the main street. He told me that he didn't even remember making the conscious decision to be there. "It's as if I just find myself there," he'd often say.

For the next several hours, until four or five a.m., Tim would peruse scores of adult magazines and view adult videos in the small viewing stalls. More likely than not, though he didn't think of himself as gay, he'd have anonymous sex with another man in one of those rooms.

Driving home, filled with overwhelming guilt and shame because he was a Christian and a member of a thriving local church, he would stumble into the house in a mental stupor. His wife, a heavy sleeper, was often still asleep as he slipped into the shower. He'd dress, eat breakfast, look over his lesson plans and head out the door for a day's teaching. This happened two or three times a week. It had been going on like this for years.

Tim was able to keep up this routine without anyone knowing. His wife, people in his church, even the men in his Tuesday morning discipleship group never suspected anything. He had become that good at hiding it all, being who and what he needed to be here, there, and everywhere, whatever each situation demanded. He had become a spiritual chameleon. An expert in deceit and cover-ups, Tim had compartmentalized his behaviors, his heart, and his entire life, including his relationships.

We've seen that men struggling with sexual sin are, at deeper levels in their lives, God-haters and idol-makers. A third element that goes on under the surface in the men who come into our office is that they are accomplished *game-players*, juggling all the seen and unseen parts of their lives. I see this game-player category in virtually everyone who struggles with sexual sin, but more so with believers. Why? Because in the church, struggles are kept secret from others as the pressure of appearances takes over. You are accepted if you have it all together; but you are viewed differently if you admit you have problems or difficulties. This is especially so when the struggle involves sex, with its attendant shame and guilt. In other words, Christians believe they should not have these problems. The church should not be this way, but oftentimes the "culture" of a church creates this relational dysfunction.

A number of years ago, this was made clear to me when our ministry placed carefully-worded ads in local newspapers and magazines, aimed at those who might be questioning what was going in their lives. The short ads would say something like, "Porn Struggle? Help Is Available" or "Gay and Unhappy? God Cares" or "Does Porn Have a Grip on You? There's Hope for You." When we ran those ads, we could get up to forty calls a day. We no longer run them but it sometimes still amazes me that we could have all four lines of our office phones lit up from callers seeking help.

As I talked with people who responded to these ads, I noticed something: A good number who called were non-Christians, but the ad spoke to them with some kind of clarity and hope anyway. One of the verses that has always been a foundation for our outreach is Proverbs 14:13, "Even in laughter the heart may ache." No matter how much people's lives look put together as they bask in their sexual freedom, there can still be a lot of pain and hurt underneath—even in an unbeliever!

I realized something else about those who initially came to us as unbelievers. If men came into our ministry, joined one of our Bible study/support groups, and then eventually came to a first-time, saving knowledge and faith in Christ, they often had a much better prognosis for dealing with their sexual sin biblically and sincerely. They had a healthier journey of growing in Christ and "putting off" their sexual sin than did believers who came to us after living disjointed, compartmentalized lives for many years.

How could that be? First, you've got to realize that, if you are a believer dealing with struggles like Tim the teacher, no one may know about your hidden struggles because you've designed it that way! Maybe no one even suspects the deep waters of your heart in this area and the efforts you make to keep it all working. People can go on for years with these heart-crushing, life-devastating behaviors. No one in your life may ever catch on, and you're worse off because of it. If you are ever going to deal with your heart with integrity, you will have to unlearn all the coping mechanisms you've developed to function in both worlds—your sin-oriented, secret world as well as your "Christian" world.

We have a wonderful man named Bob Heywood on staff in our national office in Philadelphia. He disciples men and works with some of our small groups. His is an amazing story of how the Lord broke into his heart over a dozen years ago, as he lived one of these game-playing, compartmentalized lives. Bob talks about the way his half-hearted Christian life was able to coexist for so long with his sexual addiction. Bob was an active elder at his church. He attended every meeting. He led worship, taught, and preached regularly at his church. But he had hidden problems that were compounded by the fact that he was able to get away with living a double life. Bob says, "As I began giving in to this temptation, I realized I was getting in way over my head. I felt like I couldn't stop. I'll never forget when I came to what I now consider the worst soul-deadening conclusion ever in my life. And that was, 'Maybe I can do both. Maybe I can be a leader in the church and look at porn at the same time.' After all, I was already getting away with it."

When Bob teaches and shares his testimony now, he often uses Proverbs 7:13–18 to describe his experience. In that passage, Solomon describes the way a prostitute taunts and seduces a young man.

> She seizes him and kisses him,
>   and with bold face she says to him,
> "I had to offer sacrifices,
>   and today I have paid my vows;
> so now I have come out to meet you,
>   to seek you eagerly, and I have found you.

I have spread my couch with coverings,
    colored linens from Egyptian linen;
I have perfumed my bed with myrrh,
    aloes and cinnamon.
Come, let us take our fill of love till morning;
    let us delight ourselves with love."

Bob uses this vivid picture to say that he was more like the prostitute than the seemingly innocent victim of someone's charms and seduction. Bob will tell you that for years he did what the prostitute did—he "offered sacrifices and paid vows," thinking this would take care of his spiritual problem and relieve him of guilt and shame. In other words, he did all the Christian stuff—went to church, read his Bible, prayed, put money in the offering basket, etc.—just as the woman in the passage carried out her religious activities. At the same time, he spent twenty years viewing adult videos. Bob's Christian life had become a works-oriented, graceless world where doing was more important than being. His carefully crafted façade allowed him to function in two worlds and fool everyone because he looked really good—at least, on the outside.

THE DECEPTIVE EASE OF LIVING A LIE

It's much easier to spot other kinds of life-dominating struggles in someone's life than it is to spot someone's hidden sexual sin. Consider the person with a drinking problem. How might you recognize that something is going on? Well, you might smell alcohol on his breath frequently. You might observe him "high" or inebriated. He might miss work due to a hangover. When I was in high school, I had an English teacher who was known as a real party animal. His life of excess was legendary around the school. He missed teaching his classes at least once every two months, due to what people were sure was an inability to get back in the classroom on some Mondays. Every time the substitute teacher showed up, we all rolled our eyes and said, "He's been on a binge again." Everyone knew exactly what was going on, even the students.

Or consider people who have a spending compulsion or gambling addiction. They might lose their home because of their debts. They might live beyond their means in big ways. When I graduated from high school, I got a job with the post office making twelve dollars an hour. In 1973, when gas cost a mere forty cents a gallon, that was pretty good pay! I was able to move to my own apartment and buy a new F-100 pick-up truck—a $5,000 purchase back then. However, as good as that job was, if I had bought a new Rolls Royce, someone would have said, "Whoa, wait a minute, what's going on?"

When it comes to sexual sin, though, men can live for years without anyone knowing how they're misusing sex. The secret nature of sexual sin allows it to go on for years without anyone ever knowing. Therein lies its deepest power to do soul and heart damage. It can lead to dozens of years of being a game-player, even as a Christian man. How does it happen? Easy. We learn to compartmentalize, that is, to wall off many parts of our lives early on. It can begin even in late childhood and be set in place by the mid-teen years. We deal with the people around us on an "as needed" basis. We can be this person over here, that person over there. And the person, even as a Christian, who learns to do that at age fifteen is soon the person doing that at twenty-five, thirty-five, forty-five, or fifty-five! I know this because men come in our office in their forties and fifties who have been playing the Christian game for years, keeping the rubbish hidden. It's a grueling feat. It's a wonder so many men can carry it off as long as they do.

Being a game-player can be exhausting. But one of the most deadly consequences of learning how to live with a pornified heart is the inevitable corrosion that takes place in our hearts over years.

The problem, though, is that you won't know that your own heart is decaying! You may be the last to know.

THE REAL EFFECTS OF A CORRODED HEART

Several years ago my family lived in a large, rambling four-story house built around 1920. It was a neat old house in one of the first suburbs of Philadelphia, where well-to-do center-city folks had once built summer homes. It even had servants' quarters on the top floor. One day I was taking a bath in the original cast-iron, claw-footed bathtub. I noticed the drain in a way I hadn't before. As I looked more intently, I saw it was really corroded. The thought hit me that I could probably poke the drain very gently with my finger, and it might just disintegrate. I did—and it did! So many years of debris had run through that drain that it had rotted what had once been a shining new steel filter. It's the same way with sexual sin and our hearts. Perhaps you have a small sense of the state of your soul in all this—that it's corroded, decayed, and been dead for years. But that's not all that a corroded heart looks like.

Our sexual sins not only cause our hearts to go dead, but they also keep us from being who and what we should be as men, husbands, and fathers. Due to years of sexual temptations and unforsaken sins, our neglected hearts will rob everyone in our lives of something! There are at least three ways that this happens.

First, a continued history of failures, a commitment to playing games with these issues and with the Lord, and a commitment to silence will rob you of your effectiveness as a man of God, as a husband, and as a father. It will rob you of the gospel words you're called to speak on a regular basis to your own heart and to the hearts of those closest to you. You can no longer preach the gospel to yourself with authority. It falls on deaf ears. You cease to believe it for yourself, even though you may go through the motions of acting like you believe it. This can be true even if you are in ministry.

Think about it. You lose your bout with Internet porn on a regular basis. You're filled with guilt and shame most of the time, with the harsh realization that you're living in defeat all the time. Now, are you going to be engaged emotionally and practically the way you should be with your wife? Are you going to be proactive in speaking into her life and your children's lives the way you know Gods wants? Probably not. You know the reality of your record, and it's zapped your relational strength, vitality, and integrity. You've come to see yourself as a fake, a phony, a sham.

A sentence in the foreword to *The Westminster Confession of Faith* applies here. This document was drawn up around 1650 to summarize all that the Bible teaches. In the foreword, Puritan clergyman Thomas Manton wrote, "Religion was first hatched in families, and there the devil seeketh to crush it."[20] Unfortunately, a neglected heart is one of the ways the Evil One is crushing the effectiveness of husbands and fathers in our churches. The terrible result is that an increasing number of men in our churches live double lives like Bob Heywood did, projecting a false image of strength on the outside while they are struggling with rottenness on the inside. The Evil One holds our histories and our guilt and shame over our heads to render us ineffective in shepherding our families. The people we are called to love and nurture the most lose out. They need our presence, but they don't have it as they should.

Second, this heart-neglect robs men of their confidence in, love for, and excitement about things of God, especially about the gospel. How could it not? When you know deep down what's going on in your heart, how you've been taken captive by your own untamed desires—and when you know your own record of defeat—it robs you of the love for the gospel you once had. But as men we can go on acting as if everything's okay. We continue our jobs and roles as spiritual leaders, husbands, and fathers, faithfully trying to fulfill all of our church commitments. But it all has a hollow ring to it. And, if we are honest with ourselves, we know exactly why, even if no one else does.

How connected are you going to be to others in this situation? Let's say that on Monday you had your bout with porn and masturbation again. You confessed it to God and made another vow. Then comes your Tuesday night deacons' meeting. Of course you're going to go. You'll show up. But is your heart going to be engaged? Maybe it will, but maybe not. And if not, you'll fake it. My guess is that you're going to be in your recovering, bargaining cycle with God, still getting over your last defeat.

Or, after your fall into sin, you notice that your calendar says you've got your missions committee meeting coming up. You'll go to the meeting—you're a guy and it's written down to go, so you'll go. But is your heart going to be in it? It's doubtful. You're there more out of duty than anything else. Your joy is gone. The things that once brought you joy and gave you a sense of being used by God—in fact, most things in your Christian life—have become one big heart-less obligation. Am I right?

Third, our unaddressed struggles, our sexual idols and compulsions also rob God! How do they do that? To pick up on Scotty Smith's words, they—we—rob God of the adoration, attention, affection, and allegiance of which he alone is worthy. The counterfeit sexual idols we bow to vie for a deep place in our hearts, a place where only God was meant to dwell. The ongoing indictment against Israel in the Old Testament was that they had forsaken God to forge gods of their own making or to adopt the gods of foreign peoples.

So, does your continual inaction, resignation, and inattention to your heart rob God? You bet. Do they rob you and those around you? Absolutely. *They keep you from being fully available to God and others.* They rob the body of Christ in a very real way. Your secret sexual idolatries, your addictions, and your compulsions keep you from being who you were called to be. In our addictions, our hearts seek attachments that cripple our image-bearing capabilities and the exercise of our gifts to bless others. This is one of the saddest, most damaging consequences of our hidden sin—everyone loses out!

I really like the book *Addiction and Grace*, a classic on understanding the source and power of our compulsions and addictions. It's the book I have marked up most, next to my Bible. In it, author Gerald May talks about the life-robbing aspect of our compulsions and addictions, whatever form they may take. Those things that privately hold us captive always have a communal effect. He writes:

> I have now come to believe that addiction is a separate and even more self-defeating force that abuses our freedom and makes us do things we really do not want to do. While repression stifles desire, addiction *attaches* desire, bonds and enslaves the energy of desire to certain specific behaviors, things, or people.
>
> These objects of attachment then become preoccupations and obsessions; they come to rule our lives. . . . Moreover, our addictions are our own worst enemies. They enslave us with chains that are of our own making and yet that, paradoxically, are virtually beyond our control. Addiction also makes idolaters of us all, because it forces us to worship these objects of attachment, thereby preventing us from truly, freely loving God and one another.[21]

By our "attachments," May means anything our hearts attach to for some sense of life. Now, you can form an unnatural and destructive attachment to many things—to food, alcohol, prescription drugs, money, exercise, entertainment, etc. They can be things that God meant for our good or that he provided for us to enjoy but that have become a vice or have become "spoiled." That's what C. S. Lewis said evil was: good, spoiled. As you read this book, you are probably most concerned about where your sexual "attachments" have led you, the way they have come to rule your life and to take on an energy and force of their own, almost a life of their own. Hopefully, you are somewhat aware of how these things, as May said, prevent you from loving and serving God and the body of Christ. Don't you think, in your loss of hope, your preoccupation with self, and your unwillingness to move forward, that Satan has you just where he wants you?

This robbing effect can also impact other, more practical aspects of our Christian life. A guy in a support group once told me about one consequence of his sexual addiction. "John, I haven't tithed in years. I can't keep up with my sex addiction and tithe too. It costs too much, and I've spent too much money on it. In the beginning I looked mostly at free porn, but once I got hooked, I began to rack up hundreds of dollars a month in subscription fees and live chat lines." This is not uncommon. Although the vast majority of porn websites are free (70–80%), they are commonly used as "bait and switch" sites to get viewers to subscribe to premium pay sites.[22]

When I talk with pastors and church leaders about what it might look like to have the men in their congregations freed up from all this, I sometimes mention that some men are in financial bondage to their sexual sin. That usually gets the pastor's full attention! What pastor wouldn't want men freed up to be giving back not only emotionally and spiritually with their engaged hearts but also with their resources? But this won't happen automatically or instantaneously; we have to intentionally work at making our churches redemptive places of hope and help for sexual sinners and strugglers of all types. When we do that, anything is possible.

WHAT REAL CHANGE LOOKS LIKE

There's more to the story, though, about the guy who hadn't tithed in years so that he could finance his addiction. As this man attended one of our groups, he came to believe the gospel more deeply. He began to want to give up his addictions and sexual idols. Eventually, he started making small steps of faith and repentance as God met him in his brokenness in some new and amazing ways. One day, several months later, he told me, "I've cheated the Lord too many years by spending money on all these things. I want to start giving back. Who should I give it to?" I knew he was a member of a local church, so I told him he should first give there. Later that week he told me that he had written a check for $5,000 to the church. Resuming his giving for the first time in years, he's continued to tithe regularly now.

Some people might be tempted to call my friend's giving "guilt money." I assure you, though, it was anything but that! As he started to live out of God's gospel love and grace, he was transformed like Zacchaeus in Luke 19. As Jesus became more important to him, his heart started to come to life too. Remember, Zacchaeus was not only hated because he was a tax collector but also because he was a "chief" tax collector. This means he probably cheated and stole more than anyone else. But, when Zacchaeus's heart was changed after doing very personal business with Jesus, he said, "Behold, Lord, the half of my goods I give to the poor. And if I have defrauded anyone of anything, I restore it fourfold" (Luke 19:8). Zacchaeus's new and radical generosity is proof of a transformed heart.

That's the power of the gospel, and it's a thrilling thing to watch in the life of a man or woman. It's what has kept me in this ministry for thirty years! It's also a clear demonstration of the biblical principle of "putting off" and "putting on" (Ephesians 4). In this case, one of the "putting off" behaviors of the man in our Bible study was to stop acting out in sexually inappropriate and sinful ways—and to stop spending his money on those activities. His "putting on" wasn't just to stop robbing God and others as he had for years; it was now giving of his time and personal resources, like Zacchaeus. This was the fruit of repentance in his life.

In these last chapters, I've explained what years of heart neglect regarding sexual sin can do to you. It can make you a God-hater, an idol-maker, and a game-player as a believer. As I've reflected on the people who have come into our ministry over the years and thought about their stories, I realized something humbling. I said to myself, "Freeman, that's who *you* are by nature. Without Christ, on any given day you're a God-hater, an idol-maker, and a game-player too. It's the temperament of every sinful heart. That's why I need Jesus, not just to clean me up or improve me. I need him to do radical heart surgery on me . . . every day! And not just in nice, pretty, safe ways, but in deep-seated, ruthless ways! I'm just like all those guys who come to us for help."

I said earlier that it's amazing how many men can carry off the deceit and game-playing for so long. But it's also a miracle when God, through the Holy Spirit, begins to break in. Then, he often gives us a sense of our desperate state of heart, as he did to the Prodigal Son as he hungered and walked among the pig troughs in Luke 15.

In the years I've been working in this field, I've been blown away again and again when a new person comes into our ministry, because God is usually behind it. As I sit there listening to that guy pour out his heart and tell me his story, often for the very first time, I'm humbled again by the fact that God cares for and pursues rotten sinners like us. You know, it's never too late for God to do a new work in your heart. You have to believe that! It's the story of the gospel. And when that something new begins to happen, it will change not only you but all your past perceptions of who Jesus is and what he wants to do in and with you.

We once had a guy attend one of our groups who had led a very secret life of bondage to his sexual idols and addictions. One day, about six months after he started attending, I asked people to share what God was teaching them. He piped up and said, "I'm learning that Jesus isn't just a self-improvement program, like I've thought of him for years. He wants to do much more in my life than just improve it—he wants to change me by changing my heart." I was amazed—and so thankful! He was beginning to really understand who Jesus is and what he does in us.

Real change isn't measured just by what we stop doing. It's always measured in character change; whereas your former preoccupation with yourself robbed others, but now you begin to be more interested in others than yourself. You see yourself wanting to bless others, desiring their good and not just your own. You no longer hide what you are doing; instead, you are increasingly open with others about your struggles and faults. As one man said to me about his decades of hidden sexual struggles: "I've been a liar all my life." But now, he is learning how to be a truth-teller, to his wife and to everyone he knows. Character grows when we live for God and serve others. One of the ways God starts to change us is to move us to start dealing with our sexual idols. You may be thinking, *Okay, I see myself in all that you've described. That's me.* Maybe you know deep down that you, too, have become a God-hater, idol-maker, and game-player. But you're thinking, *Okay, John, where's the hope in my hopelessness? What now?*

What does it take to want to start walking in repentance and find the help you know you desperately need? How do you get there? What is the path to freedom? How do you start to live with sexual integrity when you know you don't have the human resources to do so? You have to be willing for God to do something new and to begin to see yourself as you've never done before.

FOR REFLECTION AND DISCUSSION

1. How have you managed to hide your hidden struggles so that no one knows about your battles with sex? What do you have to do to work at keeping it all a secret?

2. What are the places in your life where you are living a compartmentalized life? What effect does it have on you to be a "game-player"?

3. Can you identify those people or places in your life where you are "robbing" others? How do you think that has affected them?

Chapter 5

Getting Real and Beginning to Live with Integrity

My cell phone rang around 10 p.m. Sam had left our support group meeting about an hour before. He said he was calling from the hospital emergency room. He had been in a car accident, sort of. He was okay—only a few scratches, nothing serious. Sam had a newer car and something like ten airbags deployed at once, saving his life. "I just wanted you to know what happened—and that I did it on purpose. I ran my car into a bridge abutment to kill myself. I just wanted to die."

I was stunned. I said, "Boy, I'm glad you're okay, but something big must have happened for you at the meeting tonight. Sounds like you were pretty distressed."

Sam went on to explain in a vivid way what had happened. Driving home from the meeting that night, he had realized for the first time that pornography and all of his sexual stuff weren't even the real problem. They were just the tip of the iceberg. As he reflected on that, he saw his problems more clearly than ever. What had brought him to the group just a few months ago—the actual porn and acting out behaviors—he now realized had long functioned as a fist in God's face for all the ways God had failed him—all the unanswered prayers, all the ways God had seemed not to come through for him.

But Sam had also become aware of something else. In a moment of God-given insight, he grasped for the first time that what had brought him to the group was just symptomatic of some very messy and complex issues, none of which had to do with the things he did to get himself in trouble. He said, "I saw down that long tunnel and realized how far I had to go. I felt a new kind of lostness. I knew I didn't have the ability or resources to get there. In that moment, I lost all hope. It was too much, too painful. I just wanted it to all end."

I want you to know that what Sam began to see about his life and the function of all his coping mechanisms *is* what has to happen to men regarding their porn and sexual compulsions—just, hopefully, not that dramatically! You must begin to see that it's not that TV screen, that scantily clad woman, that muscle-bound guy, that computer screen or that pop-up beckoning your heart that's the real problem.

When Sam saw the scope of what was going on beneath the surface, he lost hope. He became overwhelmed, and that's when people can spiral into despair and anguish. A counseling professor once told my seminary class that people usually don't become suicidal by lying depressed and non-functional in bed for months. Rather, it's often when you get a little glimmer of hope and begin to see the road you need to travel but then realize you don't have the strength, will, or skills necessary to travel that road. You see your future as bleak. Regarding suicidal feelings, my professor also said that people normally don't have "nervous breakdowns"—they have "resource breakdowns." How will I get where I need to go? What will it take? Who will help? It all becomes heart-crushing. This is what happened to Sam.

I talked with Sam into the night, encouraging and reassuring him. I agreed that he didn't have the resources to "get there" all by himself. No one does outside of Christ. I talked with him about how the Lord would be intimately involved with him in all that needed to happen—and that I and other guys in the group were there for him. We'd walk with him in this new journey. However, he had to continue to open up his heart and life to those who could come alongside him.

What does it take to get out of the porn/sex-gone-wrong pit? *You have to start getting ruthlessly honest before God and a few other people about what's going on in your life and soul.* I will talk more about this in a later chapter, but as I raise the issue now, let me venture to guess that this idea may strike terror in your heart. This, however, is the beginning of the pathway to freedom. Of course, many have absolutely no experience in doing this or even attempting it. You've wished away your struggles and temptations hundreds of times. You've hoped it would all just go away, resolve itself, disappear. But, really, that's all just been a mind-game you've played for far too long, all alone in your recliner, isolated in your pit.

THE TUPPERWARE SYNDROME

If you're like most guys, you've learned, through practice amid your long-term feelings of hopelessness, to push away any thoughts of trying to handle it all. This is especially true when you glimpse the ugliness of it all, the foulness of what's going on in your heart. And in doing so, you've become a victim to what I've come to call the "Tupperware Syndrome." Those of you over fifty probably remember those brightly colored plastic food containers in which you placed your leftovers. Unlike today's see-through containers, back then you couldn't see what was inside. What was under that lid was often a mystery.

Early on in my marriage, we used a lot of Tupperware. Sometimes, when I would go to the fridge hungry and curious about what was in those containers, I would lift a lid just enough to see what was inside, only to find out that it should have been thrown away days ago. It was quite evident with the first whiff that whatever was in there was spoiled. It stank so much that there was no way I would want to eat it. So, what did I do? Did I walk over to the garbage disposal and empty it, like people would normally do? No way. I pushed that stinky stuff back into the fridge and thought, *I'll let my wife deal with that.* I didn't have the time or energy to handle it. I deemed it too dark, ugly, and unpleasant to deal with. So I left it right where I found it!

Like me and like Sam, it may be that when you think about your sexual struggles, you feel you lack the resources to deal with them. This is especially true when you get a glimpse of how complicated and ugly it may be, and how it's a bigger mess than you originally thought. Once again, the Evil One has you just where he wants you—in despair and unbelief. But, hey, this has become your home. It's all too familiar.

We often can't handle the truth about ourselves. I love the words to the old hymn, "I Need Thee, Precious Jesus," written in the mid-1800s. One line says, "I need Thee, precious Jesus, for I am full of sin. My soul is dark and guilty, my heart is dead within."[23] But, if I am honest, there is a part of me that also hates these words on some level. Why can't we just own the fact that this is most of us, most all the time? What keeps us from the honest realization that we're in desperate straits naturally and functionally, in both heart and life?

What keeps us from being ruthlessly honest with God or others about our deep struggles? There are many reasons. For starters, we fear that if we are honest with someone else, our whole world will collapse. Also, that kind of honesty makes us feel exposed and more vulnerable than we've ever been. We wonder if our image and reputation as Mr. Nice Guy, Mr. Have-It-All-Together, or Mr. Christian will be shattered. But, in reality, I think there's always something else going on in us deeper down—something much simpler and more foundational.

What keeps most of us in the prison of self-protection, never admitting to God or anyone else the state of our hearts, is our unbelief that we have a heavenly Father who has all the goods on us and yet extends mercy and compassion to us anyway! Knowing our own miserable records, we have ceased to believe—or maybe never believed in the first place—that God cares more about us personally than he does our performance records as men. We imagine God looking at our list of miserable failures and never seeing past them to see our misery and despair. A just and holy God will have nothing to do with us because deep down we all know the reality of our botched attempts at saving ourselves regarding sex. We know we stand condemned, and we don't believe God wants to or can do anything other than judge us and find us guilty. But, this is a skewed view of God that only keeps us stuck in our hopelessness. Our belief that God is more interested in condemning us than helping us is what ultimately causes us to hide from him. Why do I think that? Because this is the way I tend to treat other people. Let me explain.

I "point-and-shoot" my mental camera at my coworkers, my staff, my friends, my family—all those closest to me— when they sin against me. I do it when they have disappointed me, hurt me, or failed me. I take that picture and store it away in my mind. Then, the next time I'm called to trust that person, depend on him, or get close to him, my knee-jerk reaction is to retrieve that photo and say, "Aha! I know what you're really like. You had your chance with me and you blew it. Forget it."

That's my sinful nature. And it's also my initial gut reaction to the knowledge that someone has seen the less-than-perfect side of *me*. We think of God as a cosmic Santa Claus, making a list, checking it twice, trying to find out who's naughty and nice. But, it's no surprise that we're the ones who aren't so nice! But be encouraged. This is not a true picture of God and how he sees you. God already knows the deep stuff about you—the stuff that would make you run for cover if you thought anyone might find out. Nothing will surprise him, so quit fooling yourself. If you have given your life to Christ, and you know that it is his death on the cross that cancels your sin, then even your sin and sinful heart aren't deal-breakers for God, even though you continue to struggle, and fail, with sexual sin. But it is your commitment to self-sufficiency and trying to work it all out on your own that will keep you from walking with him!

You see, when God thinks of us as his children, he does take out a picture, but it's not of us. It's of his Son, Jesus Christ. His image has now been superimposed on ours. The One who has done all things well and in harmony with God's will has his face pasted over my photo, the image of one who has done nothing well. The One who is without sin, pure and blameless, with a record we'll never possess except by faith, has substituted his image for ours. The loveliest image inserted over the most unlovely is what makes us lovely!

Can you believe that? It's true. It's the gospel. And that truth— that Jesus is "for us," in our place, his record of perfection and obedience applied to our accounts—is how God sees us as his children, even his hard-hearted, rebellious children. While God knows that at heart I am a God-hater, idol-maker, and game-player, he deals with me as if I am none of these because he is willing to treat his Son in my place as if he were all three! I may be one whose past record stinks. My present temptations may include ongoing "pulls" to pursue the counterfeit intimacy that sexual sin offers. Despite it all, God sees me through the record of his beloved Son!

You have to believe this to begin to deal with your stuff. You won't take the step to be honest with God or anyone else until you see yourself as someone Jesus wants and as someone he would love to spend time with despite your miserable record! Only the gospel can give you this confidence, and only the gospel can give you the courage to get real, knowing you have nothing, ultimately, to lose, but everything to gain.

You have a heavenly Father who knows when you're avoiding and where you're running, but he is waiting for you like the Prodigal Son's father was always waiting. Only when you realize this will you have the courage to take those first steps into the light and begin again. God is for us in Jesus Christ. He gives us the will and desire to look to the cross and his work there as we begin to be honest.

But be warned: looking to the cross of Christ as you consider yourself and your sin will both embolden and disrupt you!

FOR REFLECTION AND DISCUSSION

1. Have you ever experienced the kind of hopelessness that Sam felt at the beginning of this chapter? How does that express itself in your life? What is happening right now in your own life where you are tempted to throw in the towel and give up hope?

2. Does it make any difference in your life that God knows all the deep, dark "stuff" about you—and yet still desires a relationship with you? Does that knowledge impact you negatively or positively?

3. What are the things that keep you from being totally honest with God? With those who know you? As a first step, can you just begin to be honest with God, holding nothing back?

Chapter 6

Letting the Gospel Disrupt You and Dispel the Lie that You're Powerless

I first met Jim, a business professional in his mid-forties, as we happened to enter the door at the same time at my church. We introduced ourselves, exchanged greetings, and did some general chit-chat. It wasn't much beyond the typical, "Good morning. How are you?" but I did learn that Jim had been a member of the church for about fifteen years.

I thought Jim might be someone to get to know since he was not involved in our ministry. Because most of my life involves speaking, teaching, and ministering to men with all forms of broken sexuality, my wife was concerned about my need for well-rounded relationships centered on Christ and not just people's problems. She had urged me, "Can't you just try to make some friendships with 'normal' guys?" (She doesn't realize there are no "normal" guys!)

Because Jim seemed like a guy I could get to know, one morning I asked if he would like to have lunch sometime. He readily accepted and we made a lunch appointment.

A few weeks later at lunch, about fifteen minutes into the meal, Jim began talking to me about his Internet porn problems. (I tend to forget how many people know what I do for a living.) Now it clicked as to why he had so readily accepted my invitation. So I took a deep breath, thinking, *Okay, God, I'm your man, he's your man, and you own the time here. This is of you.* I thanked Jim for sharing his story with me and tried to gently go deeper with a few probing questions.

"How long has all this been going on?" I asked.
"For about ten years," he told me.
"How often?" I probed.
"Two or three times a week, for a few hours at a time," he confessed.
"Have you ever spoken with anyone about this?" I pressed on.
"No."
"Are you in a men's group in the church?"
"Yes."
"Does this issue ever come up there?"
"No."
"Would you ever be willing to bring it up and share your own situation?" I asked.
With a look of dread, I got a resounding, "Never."

As Jim went on talking, I was hit by how matter-of-fact, unemotional, and detached he seemed as he spoke. Eventually, he began to back-pedal, minimizing what he was doing, both its hold and its impact on him. I don't normally react quite this bluntly, but at one point I said, "Hold it! Right now, I hear addict-speak coming out of your mouth. You're in a worse state than you can imagine."

I went on to try to help him see the numbing effect of it all and how that was reflected even as he was talking to me. I tried to pursue it further, this time more gently, pointing out that he had become intoxicated by his own addiction. I stressed his need to do something redemptive to get out of the pit he had dug for himself. I talked about the heart-deadening, desensitizing impact of his years of routines, accumulated habits, silence, and isolation. Finally, I offered to get together with him again.

It's been over a year now and I'm still waiting. I don't think he'll be having lunch with me again anytime soon.

Even as I share this story it saddens me. While I was glad Jim opened up to me that one time, he was not convinced of the dangerous state of his heart and life. He was willing to confess to me, perhaps seeing me as someone "safe" to acknowledge his behavior to. He was somehow led to a moment of honesty, but he had not let his encounters with the gospel disrupt his soul. He still was invested in keeping up the pretense. As a result, he didn't yet have eyes to see what was happening in his heart and life.

Sometimes people confuse the act of admitting their problem with doing something positive about it. Yes, disclosing must be the first step, but it cannot and must not stop there. If it does, it can only give you a false sense of doing something positive. Blurting it all out isn't necessarily redemptive; it can serve a false purpose of just getting it off your chest.

Perhaps your own feelings of guilt and shame have led you momentarily to let someone in to your hidden world, but it's never gone further than that. The truth is, our nature is to flee and hide when it comes to our sin and the guilt and shame that accompany it. It was our first parents' response to being exposed. Adam and Eve hid and covered themselves with leaves. Things haven't changed much for the fallen human heart.

Maybe you know about Dr. Phil, the television psychologist. I don't watch the show much, but I've been surprised at some of the things he's said with which I totally agree. He says that only what is admitted can be changed. That's actually scripturally accurate. The psalmist put it this way:

> For when I kept silent, my bones wasted away
>   through my groaning all day long.
> For day and night your hand was heavy upon me;
>   my strength was dried up as by the heat of summer. *Selah*
> I acknowledged my sin to you,
>   and I did not cover my iniquity;
> I said, "I will confess my transgressions to the Lord,"
>   and you forgave the iniquity of my sin. *Selah* (Psalm 32:3–5)

Do you understand what he is saying here? Confession is always the *beginning* of repentance and change. In other words, you can't have repentance and change without genuine confession.

Dr. Phil makes another point that is consistent with the teaching of the Bible. He says that the best predictor of future behavior is past behavior. This too is true. We'll probably keep making the same destructive choices and do what's necessary to keep our inner and outer worlds separate *unless* something happens to derail us, break us, and get us going in another direction. But, what Dr. Phil doesn't tell you that the Bible does is that this is a vital part of the work of the Holy Spirit. This is what Paul tells the Christians in the city of Thessalonica, a place that was no stranger to rampant sexual sin. At the beginning of his first letter to them, he tells these believers why he is thankful for them. He is confident about God's saving work in them "because our gospel came to you not only in word, but also in power and in the Holy Spirit and with full conviction" (1 Thessalonians 1:5). Thankfully, this is what God does by his Spirit: he powerfully disrupts our lives in order to get our attention.

In our ministry I always tell people (most often family members with someone in their lives who is a sexual train wreck) to pray for both a "holy" disruption and a "wholly" disruption orchestrated by

God. By this I mean to pray for the friend or loved one to be "holy" disrupted by an awesome, mercy-driven encounter with the gospel, maybe like never before. By "wholly" disrupted, I mean to pray for circumstances to crumble and decay in their lives, so that they call out to God and others in desperation in a totally new way. These kinds of prayers are really quite dangerous. Both ways of praying involve being disrupted by God on the road they're traveling; the former depends on God's mercy toward this person, while the latter involves the sovereign movement of God in the events of his life.

Let me give you an example. I know a man who was once in a fifteen-year committed gay relationship. Just a few days apart, his father was in an auto accident and his partner was in a boating accident. He spent the next month traveling between rehab centers, caring for the two men he best loved in his life. During this time he began to read a Bible that his partner's mother had given him some years before. He'll tell you now, twenty years later, that in his Manhattan apartment, between his Marlboros and martinis, he found Jesus—or rather Jesus found him. This began a major disruption in his soul that led him to begin attending a local church. Soon he was converted. This led to some amazing life changes as God began to get hold of his heart and all its compartments. He later attended seminary and is now married—to a woman. The gospel had so disrupted him in some difficult and heart-sifting ways, that he was changed by God's love and mercy just where God had found him. Mercy is like that. It always is given in a discerning manner by the Giver, with the intentions of disrupting and eventually deterring someone from his current path.

If you're a man struggling deeply with your misuse of sex, you know what I mean about continuing the same old temptations, patterns, routines, and failures you think you'll never overcome. Your heart may be fatigued and discouraged, feeling nothing will ever change. For many men, sex with its chaos and mess has plagued them for as long as they can remember. One day I had a guy in my office ask me, "Why do we have so much trouble with sex anyway? Why does it seem to get us into so much trouble?" In a nutshell, sex has a unique power to bring blessing and/or harm to our hearts, to those around us, and to our relationship with God—almost more than anything else in life. Sex and our sexuality are great gifts from God, and they can be great gifts to others; but the reality is that they also can damage and destroy. I wrote earlier that sex is a much bigger force than we were ever meant to handle alone, especially once it's experienced out of bounds from God's will. Once again, this is because we use it as something we worship. Sex and the way we use or misuse it will reveal what is ruling our hearts. It will display our heart's allegiance.

In "The Way of the Wise: Teaching Teenagers about Sex," Paul David Tripp talks about the role sex plays in our hearts and lives. He says, "Sex is presented in Scripture as a principal way a person expresses his submission to or rebellion against God. . . . Human beings live out of one of only two identities: that I am ultimate and autonomous or that I am created and dependent on God. . . . It is when I am confronted with my utter inability to meet the demands of God's standards that I am also confronted with the reality and majesty of His grace. . . . Sex reveals my need of grace. God's call to sexual purity is as impossible for me to achieve without His help as it would have been for me to save myself."[24]

The humbling truth this quote reveals is that we all need ongoing rescue from ourselves in this area of our lives. And we always will! There will never be a time this side of heaven when I cease needing to be rescued from myself and the places my own evil heart goes—or wants to go, when it comes to sex. I keep thinking there will be a time when my heart will cease to want what's bad for it. But that's bad theology and childish thinking.

TEMPTATION IS NOT FAILURE

For guys who struggle with unrelenting sexual temptations, it can be so easy to lose the war before you even begin to engage in the battle! You can feel defeated at the first indication that your heart is attracted to something. This is often due to our own naïveté, immaturity, or ignorance about the nature of our hearts and the reality that there is no neutrality out there (the world) or in here (the heart). Like Tripp pointed out, my heart is never neutral: it either submits to God and his ways or it is moving in rebellion against him. My heart is fallen, as is all of creation. I am both tempted by the world and what it offers as much as my own heart and what it thinks it needs.

When our hearts feel the first pull toward something that could lead to bad choices, we often think, "Oh no, not again." It's here that many men get caught off-guard, drop out, give up, and succumb. It's almost as if we're surprised, all over again, at the reality that "sin is crouching at the door. Its desire is for you" (Genesis 4:7). I don't think this will ever change in this life. We can't forget that the pull of our hearts to go in bad directions is a normal part of day-to-day life—maybe even hour-to-hour! Let's get real. We won't ever escape the pull of our hearts toward sin on this earth. But we can learn that God provides the tools to deal with them and offers a way out before the temptations become destructive.

Martin Luther was specifically referring to sexual temptations when he wrote, "You should follow the advice of a hermit who was approached by a young man complaining of having lustful thoughts and other temptations. The old man told him, 'You can't stop the birds from flying over your head. But only let them fly. Don't let them nest in your hair.' It's all right to have these thoughts, but let them remain just that—thoughts. Don't let them grow to the point where you have to act on these thoughts."[25] More men need to learn that difference; that you can't always control where your mind and heart are pulled, but you can choose not to actively go in that direction. We need not be surprised that birds (those external and internal temptations) will always be flying overhead.

At times like this, when we're facing deep temptation and heart struggles, everything comes at us at once, making us think there is nothing else to do but give in again. We believe the lies about ourselves and the false promises held out by our temptations. Do you ever feel that way—that there's no other way to turn, but to give in? It may be hard to remember that it's a lie because we often feel it so deeply. We can be successful, gifted men in so many other areas of our lives, but when our hearts are assailed by sexual temptation, we bail. We're often reduced to wimpy guys who feel we have no choice but to give in.

I love that old TV series *The Sopranos*—at least the PG version on the A&E channel. I like that it shows the vulnerable side of some genuine tough guys who are members of a Mafia family. It was amazing to watch these hardened guys run up against situations that seemed too difficult for them. Faced with an overwhelming situation, they always reacted with the same gesture and words. They would grimace, shrug their shoulders, and say, "Whatchagonna do?" Unbelievable! Here were grown men (actually sociopathic hardened killers) reduced to helpless men, unable to make decisions.

In his classic *Mere Christianity,* C. S. Lewis talks about being overwhelmed by the odds when dealing with the lusts of our own hearts and confronts our tendency to throw up our hands in defeat. After describing the many ways the world "associate[s] the idea of sexual indulgence with the ideas of health, normality, youth, frankness, and good humour," he notes that "the lie consists in the suggestion that any sexual act to which you are tempted at the moment is also healthy and normal."[26] Is this how you act when confronted with temptation? It's also what's going on when we fall for the lies that our own hearts tell us. We give in to the lie that our lusts can't be resisted, so why even try. And then, the more we give in, we find ourselves, over time, slowly embracing the lie of the world that our lusts are really natural and healthy. We call what is wrong, right; we say what is unhealthy, is now healthy. We are now deceived by two lies. But the reality is really quite different: They can be resisted when looked squarely in the eye with the light of the gospel!

The Evil One wants us defeated, resigned, hopeless. It's where the world wants us too. Do you think many people in the world believe it's worthwhile to seek to live an obedient and holy life? They don't. I haven't encountered much support for that in the world in which we live. It's just not a priority for those around us. Sadly, the messages about how "liberating" our sexual freedom is are rampant out there. If anything, we're encouraged to just "go for it." We're egged on to indulge without considering the consequences. No one seems to have a gauge for what is healthy and what isn't anymore, sexually speaking.

In an article in a major newspaper several years ago, a psychologist wrote about the dangers of sexual addiction. But her own confused thinking and faulty foundations clouded her advice. In commenting on the proliferation of sexually explicit materials, especially on the Internet, she said something quite beyond belief—well, almost. She said there may be such a thing as too much assimilation of sexually explicit material in our lives, but who really knows how much is too much? She went on to say that viewing fifteen X-rated adult films a week would definitely be harmful—but three or four a week might be healthy and bring positive results, perhaps spicing up one's marriage! I couldn't believe what I was reading. The spiritual darkness was so blatant. This is the kind of world we live in and these are the kind of hearts we have!

What's worse, though, is that I see some of this thinking expanding even into the Christian world. The believing men in our own churches are being enticed not only to minimize the deadly effects of all this but, as Lewis stated above, to think it "perverse and abnormal" to even resist such urges. Let me give you an example. Not long ago, I was invited to speak to a men's group at a local church. About 120 men attended the Saturday morning breakfast where I was speaking on "Living as Men of Integrity in a Porn-Is-the-Norm World." As part of my talk, I discussed a passage from 1 Thessalonians in the New Testament. In that letter, Paul says, "For this is the will of God, your sanctification: that you abstain from sexual immorality; that each one of you know how to control his own body in holiness and honor, not in the passion of lust like the Gentiles who do not know God" (1 Thessalonians 4:3–5). As soon as I finished reading this verse, a young guy of about thirty jumped to his feet. His words jolted me as he yelled out, "That's crazy. God can't expect anyone to live like that anymore!"

At first, I was startled by his outburst—and the passion behind it. But then I thought to myself, *He's probably just voicing what two-thirds of the men here believe deep down in their hearts.* I didn't want to sound condemning when I responded to this man in front of the crowd, but I certainly couldn't let this one go by! "Wow," I said. "You feel quite strongly about that! But let me tell you, friend, not only does God still expect this of followers of Jesus, he never gives us standards or commands to obey that he doesn't also give us the resources and power to obey them." I went on to talk about what Paul teaches regarding the work of the Holy Spirit in us and what his presence enables us to accomplish regarding the pursuit of personal holiness.

Are you like this guy? Are you tempted to throw in the towel, thinking there will never be any victory in your fight? Are you on the verge of settling into cynicism, not only believing that you'll never get over this, but becoming more tolerant of it, maybe beginning to believe the lie that says, "What's wrong with it?" One of the best things you can do is to be honest about that with God and a few trusted friends. Open your heart up to the Lord and to your friends. Let them know where you are tempted to despair and unbelief. Let God in on the confused and fatigued state of your heart. Start to "pray" your emotions, fears, and despair instead of stuffing them away or letting them explode and control you. After all, most of us go to one of these extremes or the other. God can handle it, and so can some choice friends—if they are the right kind of friends!

I was so proud of a friend recently. Tom struggles intensely with sexual temptations and with unbelief, confusion, and despair about them. He told me it had gotten to the point that he just had to let someone in on the desperate state of his heart. So, he had called one of the elders in his church, whom he respected and who had a kind, encouraging, and realistic heart about the Christian life, and he simply set up a time to get together for coffee. I was so thankful when he told me that. More of us need to be doing this. We need to let someone we respect in on the state of our souls, someone who can see more clearly than we can. We need a community to help us process the dark stuff we are dealing with and to help us repent well.

What can give us the hope to believe that God still can and still wants to do something amazing with our struggles with sexual sin? It has to be based on how we believe he sees and deals with his children—you and me. We have to believe that because of Jesus, God sees us not as we are right now but as we're going to be. Our record of temptations and failures is wiped away, leaving only a future. God knows what kind of people we are! But part of our problem is that we fail to see ourselves in a true light. We tend toward all-or-nothing thinking. We either see ourselves as beyond repair and redemption, or we see ourselves as not that bad and our sin not that deadly!

A pastor once described the heart-reality of the average person in the average gospel-believing church, acknowledging that every church will have people in it who struggle with sexual sin as well as other life-dominating sins. He said:

When these people sit in our pews, they are in various stages of dealing with their problems. Some are denying that they have a problem. Some know they are sinning against God's law but have secretly rebelled, and live lives of hypocrisy and deception. Some are struggling with various degrees of success and failure in making the changes God requires. Others are regularly and effectively using the grace present in the gospel to lead changed lives.[27]

Do you see yourself or someone you love in this list? What a radically realistic view of the church, one that is both alarming and encouraging. But, this pastor's insight acknowledges that we're on a journey, either in a bad direction or a good one—or maybe we've come to a standstill. His words also show that we need a community to help us process our soul's discouraging elements and learn how to live a life of faith and repentance.

MORE THAN AN INFUSION OF GRACE

What enables us to progress from one stage to another, to boldly and radically be honest about the state of our hearts? It comes from knowing you've nothing to lose but everything to gain by trusting it all to Christ—trusting your hardened or confused heart, your corrupt desires, and your love for your sin, to him. It also requires trusting in the finished work of Christ for the past, present, and future *for you*—just where you may find yourself right now. It means trusting his record instead of yours. It means realizing that we all, at any given moment, are in desperate need of the grace that is found in Jesus. It's a grace that isn't manufactured or self-produced, but one that comes from above as a gift from God. Let me illustrate.

Several years ago, I was playing tennis on a very hot day. I had lost some weight recently and had failed, on this particular day, to drink much water. At one point I found myself flat on my back on the tennis court, having fainted. I tried to stand up but fainted again. My tennis partner called 911. Soon an ambulance arrived and they loaded me on a stretcher and drove full-speed to the nearest hospital.

At the hospital the doctor told me that I was dangerously dehydrated. They put in two IV drips, one in each arm, to rehydrate me. In a few minutes a nurse appeared and said, "Mr. Freeman, sometimes these small plastic IV tubes get a 'kink' in them, interrupting the steady flow of the IV solution. If you see that happening, that is, if it's not steadily flowing like it should, then just reach up and flick the tubing with your finger. That will cause it all to flow again as it should."

Isn't that how you often feel when you think about grace, about your struggles with temptation and sexual sin, and about your failures? We think about God's forgiveness and grace as if it's being "infused" into us. It's available, but it's up to us to keep it coming. We have to reach up every once in a while and give it a flick to get it flowing. But living by Christ's righteousness and record is never about it being infused into us over time, with occasional helps from us. Rather, it is *imputed* to us once and for all. It's about Christ and his record being applied to our accounts once and for all. It's believing and grasping by faith the truth that his righteousness and grace are now fully mine. Christ's perfect record of obedience has erased our scarred personal records and replaced them with his own; this has been done with all of our past, present, and future behaviors! Something is "imputed" when it has been transferred to someone's account or record because of someone else's actions or efforts. The beneficiary doesn't have to do a thing.

Let me try to explain what imputation means. In our ministry, our staff, like other missionaries, depend 100 percent on God's people to provide the resources we need to run this organization and accomplish our mission. God has been very faithful in providing our needs. I've never missed a paycheck in thirty years. But once, when I took my paycheck to my bank to deposit it, something very unusual happened. I glanced at my deposit slip and saw that it read $25,000. Now, while God has been very faithful, I knew he had not given me $25,000 for that two-week pay period! That walk back to the counter was one of the slowest walks I can remember. My feet felt like lead! To be honest, my first thoughts were something along the lines of, *Now I wonder . . . would they ever catch this?* The bank teller had made a wrong entry to my bank record and ledger. She had made a wrong calculation, and imputed it—credited it—to my account erroneously!

God never makes this kind of mistake. He offers you this grace even though he knows how dark your heart really is. He freely gives you his grace in spite of your most recent X-rated fantasy. Since he sees the cesspool that is your heart, you can't see how he can possibly forgive you again. But he does! He credits Christ's record and righteousness to our accounts, and it is never by accident or in error. It's purposeful and intentional. We don't go in and out of his grace based on our records.

But many of us are unnecessarily on a roller-coaster ride with God, one day at the top of the coaster, the next down at the bottom. Or, even worse, turned upside down again by the fickleness and inconsistency of our own hearts and actions. The truth is, we have to be disrupted to our core by God's grace for us in our worst moments. It's then, in the midst of our temptation and confusion, that we can see that we're not as powerless as we think we are. We can choose obedience, even though we feel quite powerless. Gerald May says it most clearly: "Ironically, freedom becomes most pure when our addictions have so confused and defeated us that we sense no choice left at all. Here, where we feel absolutely powerless, we have the most real power. Nothing is left in us to force us to choose one way or another. Our choice, then, is a true act of faith. We may put our faith in ourselves or in our attachments or in God."[28] In order to do this or believe this, we have to believe the gospel is "for us" in whatever stage we find ourselves.

FOR REFLECTION AND DISCUSSION

1. If you have never told anyone about your sexual struggles and failures, what do you think would have to happen to get you to the point of doing so?

2. What level of cynicism do you think you are at—becoming hardened about ever finding hope and success in your struggles, or beginning to change your opinion about what Scripture says about sexual integrity before God?

3. Do you grasp the difference between the "infusion" of grace vs. the "imputation" of grace? Since Christ's righteousness and grace have been imputed to believers, instead of having to be earned or attained, does this have any impact on you in your struggles with temptation and failure? Even if it doesn't impact you yet, how should it?

Chapter 7

Believing the Gospel Is for You and Learning to Live in the Banqueting Room

His call was one of the many that I receive, almost weekly, from pastors and other church leaders. He told me a story that is true of an increasing number of church leaders today.

Now in his mid-forties, Evan told me that he had struggled secretly with pornography since his teens. He had never quite gained "victory" over it, except for short periods of time, usually about six months to a year. He also told me that it was his practice, as an elder in his church, to take several men each year through a weekly, small group discipleship program, the kind that had grounded him as a new Christian in college. He had run these groups for men in his church for about twelve years.

In one recent group meeting, something happened to Evan that hadn't happened in years, something radical. "John," he said, "it was like I had been on auto-pilot in my life and ministry for years. Then one day, God just reached over and turned the auto-pilot off.

"I was doing the regular stuff I did with the men in the group that morning: going over our assigned Bible study, repeating our Scripture memorization, and sharing and praying. As we were studying the Scriptures together, it hit me upside the head like a ton of bricks. The gospel was for me too. After all these years it was still for me. Imagine an elder, a leader of others, coming to that conclusion and realization twenty years into ministry!"

Evan went on to explain how, while on auto-pilot, mechanically moving through life and ministry, he had lost a personal sense of the gospel being for him. He knew that this was mostly due to his recurrent temptations and failures and his choice to deal with it alone. The unresolved habits and the resulting guilt and shame had taken a devastating toll on him. He knew his ministry had become sterile and impersonal, even though it was still fruitful in men's lives and things were happening under his leadership. In that sense, he's like a lot of church leaders today: seeing just enough fruit and blessing, without always seeing the desperate state of his own soul!

But with Evan's new encounter with the gospel, he knew that things could not go on as they had. Not knowing how it might turn out, and admitting that it could very well be the end of his ministry, he opened up to a few of his trusted fellow elders about what had been going on in his life and heart for years. This breakthrough had not only radically changed how he thought about his own struggles and his walk with Christ, it gave him the courage to risk his heart with others, others who held a lot of power in his life.

In chapter 5, I talked about learning to see yourself the way God sees you—how God always looks at his children in light of the picture of his own Son, Jesus. This is how Evan began to view himself again, and it gave him the power to take new, scary, but necessary steps.

When we begin to see ourselves the way God sees us, it can give us the courage to run into God's presence with all our "stuff," no matter what it is. Knowing that we have an advocate, a mediator, a great high priest representing us and talking to the Father on our behalf, changes everything. At least, it *should*!

We need to be reminded of the continuous open invitation to rush into God's presence that we read about in Hebrews 4:14–16.

> Since then we have a great high priest who has passed through the heavens, Jesus, the Son of God, let us hold fast our confession. For we do not have a high priest who is unable to sympathize with our weaknesses, but one who in every respect has been tempted as we are, yet without sin. Let us then with confidence draw near to the throne of grace, that we may receive mercy and find grace to help in time of need.

I realize that this might be hard for you to really take in because I know from personal and ministry experience that approaching the throne of grace is not a routine matter for sexual strugglers, especially men. Too much gets in the way. Fear, anger, doubt, unbelief, guilt, and shame about our struggles and failed histories all keep us from approaching the throne. Did you get an idea from these verses about the mindset we're to have as we approach the throne? What does it say? Does it say "draw near" when we've got it all together? No. When we're repentant enough? No. When we can see, after self-analysis, just where and why we did what we did, where we stumbled? No. It says to draw near, with confidence, at the time of our *need*. When you're the most undone over yourself, your heart, or your actions. When you're a mess in all of your fear, doubt, double-mindedness, anger, guilt, and shame. Why? Because to come to God, all you need is your need. What qualifies you to do business with Jesus is a sense of your own neediness. Again, this is not natural for men. It's supernatural! It's something men must ask God for the ability to do, and then, through practice, train themselves in—often, being led by other men!

RUNNING TO THE CROSS

The throne of grace is the place we are invited to be totally honest and where we learn to be completely open. This is where we can be shockingly candid about the fact that we may not even want to give up our sin at all. There's a reason we turned to these things in the first place—they're enjoyable! At least, they are in the moment. So while our deepest desire may be freedom, there is often a large part of us that doesn't totally want to give up our sin. Gerald May talks about one particular way he deals with his double-minded heart—he actually prays *while* engaging in addictive behaviors. This may sound strange, but as he points out, this is a good way to tell if your desires or behavior has taken an idolatrous turn. In other words, if you find it hard to come to God in prayer while engaging in certain activities, it is likely you have taken a wrong turn into sin. And as May says, "At the very least, however, I can wordlessly turn to God as if to say, 'See? This is who I am.'"[29]

Once I was talking to a man who had just about given up hope that there was anything God could do about his life. The longevity of his struggles and the depth of his sin and deception were that overwhelming. At one time, in the midst of our weekly time together, I spoke with him about this idea of running to the throne of grace in the midst of a temptation or running to the cross during his time of deepest need—even in the midst of his sinful activity or after a failure. His response was pretty frank. He said, "Running to the cross—now that's a novel idea. I don't know much about that. I only know how to *slink back* to the cross . . . slink back to God after I've put enough space between me and my last acting-out thing and gathered the courage to deal with God again. I've been slinking back for as long as I can remember." Man, was he honest! This is where so many men live. In fact, I'd be surprised if you were reading this and couldn't truthfully say, "Yeah. That's me."

But, be careful here. While most of us may have experienced this, let me tell you clearly that, at best, this is a very unproductive rationale and at worst, it's "stinking thinking"! It's so theologically off-target. Where, then, does it come from? Simply put, it comes from not knowing your standing with God through his Son, Jesus Christ. It's similar to another kind of warped thinking that unresolved issues with our sin can produce—namely, *mug-shot theology*! I talked in chapter 5 about our tendency to think of God taking pictures of us at our worst. Mug-shot theology is about seeing yourself, even as a believer, in the mug shot *you've* taken of yourself when you're at your worst.

We've all read the stories of Hollywood stars caught doing something they shouldn't. Boozing. Stealing. Drugged-out. Out-of-control. Once arrested, in their mug shots they look nothing like they do on the slick magazine covers we so often see. They're haggard and worn down, almost unrecognizable. There's a sense in which you, in your failed efforts to deal with sexual sin, have come to feel at home with your own mug shot. We have mug-shot theology because we know deep down we deserve it. We know we deserve to be treated as our personal record demands. We know someone has to pay, and that often keeps us from the throne of grace and the cross because we want to pay for it ourselves. We think we ought to atone for ourselves.

What's the problem with having a slink-back mentality to approaching the throne of grace in time of need? What's wrong with having mug-shot theology? For one thing, you come to define yourself by your temptations and record of failure. What makes that so dangerous is that defining yourself in this way will neither melt your heart nor move it by God's love for you in Christ. You will know little of Christ's past, present, and future redemptive work on your behalf. You will avoid deep encounters with God where you can receive his forgiveness and grace because you're convinced either it won't last or you will be doing something to trample on it again in the near future.

As a result, your own personal worship, or maybe even public worship, becomes empty. You go through the motions. You become your own worst enemy; your urge to define yourself becomes the barrier to receiving and knowing his love. You cease to repent or even know how to walk in repentance. And most of it comes from your failure to understand what it means to be God's child in the banqueting room with Christ. Here, as in most of the Christian life, theology really does matter.

In his commentary on Romans, Martyn Lloyd-Jones goes into great detail on the first two verses of chapter five. Paul tells the believers in Rome, "Therefore being justified by faith, we have peace with God through our Lord Jesus Christ: By whom also we have access by faith into this grace wherein we stand, and rejoice in hope of the glory of God" (KJV). These verses tell us something crucial about why we often give up hope and help us understand what it is that keeps us from the cross and the throne of grace. It has to do with the word, "justified." This is the way Lloyd-Jones describes it: "Justification by faith is not a process; it is something that happens 'once and forever. . . .' Our sins are forgiven, we are clothed by the righteousness of Christ, and God declares that. . . . And what the apostle is saying here is that the moment God makes the declaration, we have had our access into this grace wherein we stand. We were outside grace before, we are now inside. So let us be very careful to give the exact translation here. 'By whom also'—by the Lord Jesus Christ—'we have had our access'—we have had it, and we still have it."[30]

Do you hear what he is saying? Our standing with God is secure. According to Scripture, we have our access to the throne room secured forever. And it's based on what Jesus has done for us. We need to get that firmly fixed in our hearts and minds! We now, all the time, have access—and it has nothing to do with us! Just what does *access* mean? To me, it means right-of-entry, availability to, ability to approach, full admittance, and admission to. No wonder we're told to approach the throne of grace with confidence! Here he is talking about the privileges and blessings that come from having our sins, our personal record of failures, covered by Christ so that we may bask in our new standing. He compares what has happened to being invited off the street into a great palace where there's a round-the-clock banquet being thrown inside.

Unable to enter before, now you're invited in. Not only that, you're provided with royal dress, a tuxedo. You now look like you belong there . . . because you do. Christ has made it possible. Once inside, you're introduced to the host of the banquet. Then you're seated at his table to partake of all the luscious elements of not only the banquet but your new ongoing place in palace life. You're now a member of the royal court. This is also the lesson of Matthew 22:1–10, the parable of the wedding feast. Except it's no parable for you anymore—it's a fact!

Lloyd-Jones continues by reminding us that, before Christ provided this access for us, God didn't look at us as his children but as those who were "under the law," and specifically as those who were rebelling against the law! But now in Christ, "God has become our Father, and He delights to see us coming to Him. He receives us, and He loves us, and He is ready and prepared to bless us, to shower His blessings upon us."[31]

You've got to grasp the truth of what he's saying here. It means everything. I don't know a sexual struggler alive, especially one who wrestles with his own sordid history of failures, who naturally believes any of this! To dare to believe that, in prayer, God actually delights to receive you, to see you coming! Wow. That's the opposite of our own gut feelings about how we should be treated. Again, the gospel is not about being treated as your record deserves; it's extended to us because of Christ. Some people say that Christ's love is unconditional. But it's not so much unconditional as it is counter-conditional. It's a love extended to us *in spite of* what we know to be true of us. The awful truth about who we are, by nature and history, hasn't changed. But

God has changed his mind about us, because of and through Jesus. Now, that's amazing!

Having access by faith into this kind of grace isn't determined by our efforts or our record. It's quite the opposite of the feelings we often have about ourselves as we stagger, fall, and stumble through life. Most importantly, it's not temporary or dependent on us. It doesn't ebb and flow. Because it is entirely dependent on Christ, whose work on the cross and in his resurrection and ascension is full and complete, our access to God and our standing before him can never be altered. Isn't this all so counterintuitive? It's an antinomy, a seeming contradiction. How can we not be "out" when we do things that would most certainly get us thrown out of the banqueting hall? But, again, let me stress that the *way* you come into God's presence and *how* you run to the cross of Jesus is as important as realizing what's been done for you. That's why Scripture says, "Let us, then, with *confidence* draw near" (Hebrews 4:16, italics added).

Sexual strugglers don't know much about this confidence thing. In chapter 4 I talked about what years of unaddressed struggles do to you, how they rob you of your confidence. Here it is again. It has robbed us of being able to "draw near with confidence." We often don't come with confidence because we mistakenly believe that we go in and out of the banqueting room. When we're doing well, we feel we're "in"; when we're not doing so well, we know we're "out." It's clear that we often base our confidence on our own self-righteous attempts to stay clean rather than on Christ and the way he has provided for us to come and draw near. Lloyd-Jones offers this helpful image: "You stand in grace; you do not slink into it; you do not creep into it; you do not crawl into it. Christ justifies us and we walk into this grace, and we stand in it . . . we are safe . . . we stand in grace firmly fixed, firmly established, secure. It is because we are not looking at ourselves and have no righteousness of our own. It is because it is all 'in Christ.'"[32]

Most of us have that slink-back mentality toward God and not an attitude of faith and repentance. Strugglers, especially those who have not come into the light with God or other people, don't usually rush into God's presence. We wait . . . and wait . . . and wait, until the opportune time. We wait until we "feel" better, until we think we have the right words, until we've worked up our courage, until we convince ourselves that this time was the last time we'd fail like that, until we've put enough distance between us and our last acting-out event, whatever form it may have taken. We wait until we've appropriately punished ourselves in a variety of ways. But, the truth is that there's usually no repentance in any of that. It's primarily a form of penance and reparation. And, that means there's little of the gospel in it.

Personally, it took me years of penance and self-atonement, even as a believer, to learn this. I had to learn that Jesus wants me at my worst, most vile moments. In my most depraved and X-rated thinking, when I'm full of unbelief, and when I've believed God's not enough and never will be—that's precisely when Jesus calls me to himself.

A REAL-LIFE PICTURE

Now you may be thinking, *John, all that theology is really heady, not real practical.* But it absolutely is practical! We've got to believe that what was true of the prodigal son's father is true for God as he waits for us! The father in that story (Luke 15) is a picture of a God who is waiting for you, watching for you, actually running *toward you* as you run toward him, continually inviting you to himself and treating you in a manner beyond your wildest imaginations. Why? Because you dared to believe what is true about God: that he receives sinners, all sinners, even the worst of sinners! That is what the father teaches us about God in this parable—that when we run to him, with our sin still clinging to us, he is already running toward us, with boundless joy at our return. Not a "Yeah, I'll take you back one more time"; but a "Let's celebrate!" If you dare to believe that and act on it, you'll find things beginning to happen, things you never expected.

Let me demonstrate what that looks like in a very practical way. Some months ago I received a frantic call from a friend. John was an elder in his church. The call came the day after Super Bowl Sunday. In tears, this father told me what had happened to devastate his world. The entire extended family had been gathered at a Super Bowl party at his house. At one point, John's brother had gone upstairs to the bathroom. While he was upstairs, he called down to ask permission to check his e-mail on John's family computer. Several minutes later John's brother called him upstairs to look at the computer. What John saw rocked his world. There on the computer, John saw some of the vilest and most graphic pornographic images he had ever seen. There were pages and pages, an array of porn websites, one after another.

John managed to keep it together the rest of the night, barely. He waited until everyone had left to speak with his ten-year-old son, Sam. He told Sam what he had found on the computer and asked if Sam knew anything about it. Had he put those images there? He got continued denials and a seemingly bewildered response from his son as to how the images might have gotten there. In a letter written to me at a later point, John described his interaction with his son in this way:

> "I'm going to ask you one more time; think before you answer. . . . Have you looked at anything you shouldn't have looked at on that screen?" He paused, looked away from me, then to the floor and said, "Yes." When I tell you I have never seen a look of shame and guilt so clearly, I am being totally honest. I did not feel anger or disappointment. I reached out and embraced my boy, whom I later learned had been sucked in by the power of Internet porn for a long time. I embraced him; he wept, I wept, and we rocked, with him on my lap, as we had done so often when he was an infant.

During the next several hours he confessed his daily habit of viewing pornography at certain "safe" hours (when our daily family pattern would allow time on the computer while others were out of sight). Other times were with friends at sleepovers, where they would use their iPod Touches, Internet-capable game consoles or smartphones to surf pornography websites. Through his tears he described how bad he felt about himself and how powerless he felt in trying to stop.

The hour was now 2 a.m. We were both beat and we were still embracing. Instead of disappointment and anger I felt relief and a deeper love for my son, who was almost asleep in my arms. Once I placed him in his bed, he fell asleep and subsequently woke several times during the next hour, calling out my name to discuss and confess some more. . . . Eventually he got everything off his chest and finally fell asleep.[33]

I don't know what you're thinking or feeling as you read this. But when I share this account with men at one of those men's breakfasts, you can hear a pin drop. I look around and see tears running down the faces of tough-looking guys. They get it! Do you?

The book of Jude helps us understand this kind of love by putting the work of Jesus into the context of both the holiness of God and the mercy of God. I realize that Jude can be difficult to digest and even a bit scary because it teaches us how serious God is about sin. But it also shows us how compassionate and merciful God is. Most of this little book, only twenty-four verses in all, talks about the ungodliness of ungodly people and the error of those who approve of the actions and hearts of ungodly people. We read, "Behold, the Lord comes with ten thousands of his holy ones, to execute judgment on all and to convict all the ungodly of all their deeds of ungodliness that they have committed in such an ungodly way, and of all the harsh things that ungodly sinners have spoken against him" (Jude 14–15). That's pretty heavy! Yet, at the end of the chapter, Jude, the brother of Jesus, says,

But you, beloved, building yourselves up in your most holy faith and praying in the Holy Spirit, keep yourselves in the love of God, waiting for the mercy of our Lord Jesus Christ that leads to eternal life. And have mercy on those who doubt; save others by snatching them out of the fire; to others show mercy with fear, hating even the garment stained by the flesh. (Jude 20–23)

What a wonderful picture of both the truth and mercy of the gospel. How can God tell us to "have mercy," "save others by snatching them out of the fire," and "show others mercy"? Because that is what he has done for us in Christ! The reason we are told to do this for others is because this is what Christ did and does for us.

Think about it. Christ left the splendor of heaven. He was separated from the most intimate, loving, eternal relationship ever known—for you. He willingly entered the mud, muck, and mire of this world—and of our hearts—to show you the love of a Father whose affection for us knows no end. I admit that what Jude says about the need to "hate even the garment stained by the flesh" used to really bother me. I've come to realize it means that God knows just who and what we are, in our sin nature and often in our own choices, in our disobedience and ungodliness—and yet he desires to have relationship with us anyway! That's the paradox and miracle of the gospel of grace. Does this stir you? It should. He loves you that much. While you may have given up on yourself, he never does.

Now, you might read all this and be ready to accuse me of *antinomianism*—that is, disregarding God's call for obedience to his law. Some may say I'm taking sin too lightly. Of course, others say I'm too hard on people and I should lighten up! Both of these accusations, though, misunderstand the nature of God's law. Think about when God's law was first given. Look at the Ten Commandments. How do they begin? "I am the LORD your God, who brought you out of the land of Egypt, out of the house of slavery" (Exodus 20:2). Do you hear what God is saying? His commandments are always given in the context of relationship. The rules that he gave to Israel are given only after he reminds them about whom they belong to and whose they are.

What a picture the Scriptures give us! Whether it's in Exodus or Luke or Jude, we find again and again a God who shows extravagant mercy to men and women who know they are sinners! Most of the guys I minister to know they've "blown it"—maybe one time too many. At least that's what a heart full of hopelessness, despair, disillusionment, and condemnation tells them. Maybe that's where you find yourself now. But God's extravagant mercy comes to us where he finds us—at our worst, most desperate, and needy moments. This is the story of God's people throughout the Bible. When I read again and again in the Bible how God's people screwed up after saying they wouldn't, I find myself saying, "I can't believe they did that again!" But God shows them mercy time and again. That's what I want you to hear.

Men who struggle deeply with sexual sins often have crafted a polished, charming, outer veneer. We don't want people to see through us, and we don't want people to see just how fragile we are. We don't want people to get too close because they might sense that we're not what we project on the outside. Walking in the dark like this for years and years, isolated and alone, changes you, and not for the better. You won't be able to receive compliments from people or receive gifts graciously, because you know you're not worthy of any of them. And you won't be able to receive the gift of God's mercy and grace when you most need it. It will feel foreign and strange—all the time. Gerald May is on target when he says, "Living into the mystery of grace requires encountering grace as a real gift. Grace is not earned. It is not accomplished or achieved. It is not extracted through manipulation or seduction. It is just given. . . . Because grace is a pure gift, the most meaningful of our encounters with it will probably come at unintended times, when we are caught off-guard, when our manipulative systems are at rest or otherwise occupied."[34] Is this true of you? Have your systems of isolation, fear, and manipulation hindered your ability to receive the grace of the gospel for you? My guess is that they have, at least to some degree.

However, can't you see how Jesus yearns to jump into all this with you? It's not too late to have him complete a search-and-rescue mission in your life. Have you asked him to do that lately? Have you come to the end of yourself and all your methods of dealing with your sexual mess? If so, that's a good thing. No, it's a great thing! In the next chapter you'll read about a pastor who was always so busy with life, job, and others that he neglected to care for his own soul. It had devastating consequences in his life. Maybe you'll identify.

FOR REFLECTION AND DISCUSSION

1. In what specific ways do you see a "slink-back" mentality in your relationship with God after big failures and sin in your life? How would you explain to someone (maybe yourself!) the difference between penance and repentance?

2. What would you have to believe about yourself and God to believe that you can draw near his throne of grace even at your worst, most X-rated moments?

3. Do you believe that Jesus longs to jump into the pit with you, and that, like the father of the Prodigal Son, he runs to you when you repent? What would be one or two things that would begin to change in your life if you acted on that belief?

Chapter 8

Learning to Deal
with Our Dark Desires

A few years ago, I received the following letter from a pastor:

John, it's been some time since we spoke. But I remember, almost twenty years ago, when you visited my church to speak on a Sunday night. It was then, on the long drive back to your hotel room, that I first told you about my dalliance in porn.

It was actually at my next church, in another state, that I developed an addiction to pornography. I tried to handle it myself, thinking that eventually I would get my life straightened out. But I stayed more isolated in my bondage than ever and, of course, it only got worse. Not knowing how to cope with the realities and pain in my life, I became an alcoholic. I continued this way for the next fifteen years, able to hide it all from everyone while continuing my pulpit ministry.

Then, two years ago, I made two suicide attempts. Amazingly, my wife and I explained each of these away as "other" illnesses that necessitated my hospitalization. I finally spoke with my elders about what had really happened and then spent time in an addiction treatment center in Phoenix. Not long after getting out of that program, I resigned as pastor.

We stayed in the same city, so at times an elder might call or meet with me, asking how I was doing. Unfortunately, I could not find any resources in my conservative Presbyterian denomination that offered any kind of ongoing help for what was, for me, a life-long, debilitating problem. Eventually things continued to deteriorate until about a year ago, when I took an overdose of medication, not really wanting to die, just wanting life and this struggle to slow down.

In the last year, however, I have begun attending SA (Sexaholics Anonymous). For the first time in my life I am finding sobriety from the hold that pornography and alcohol have had on me for years. Now, for the first time in my life, I am thinking clearly. I belong to a men's small group where all of us are dealing with the same life-crippling stuff. Most of us are now or have been pastors. Everyone knows the reality of what each of us is talking about and we address it all straightforward and head-on. No pretense. This has made all the difference in the world in my life!

I've now been able to start applying the biblical principles I learned long ago. I have a renewed understanding of God's grace and power. It's been the combination of gut-level honesty in a group where we've already lost everything or have the potential to do so, combined with authentic fellowship in a community that has had the most impact.

For over twenty-five years as a pastor and leader, I was the one who orchestrated first-aid and crisis care management in countless people's lives. There was no time, room, or honest, safe place for me to do that for myself! John, please feel free to use my story with others in church leadership if it would help. Tom

When I read this e-mail from Tom, I remembered that evening twenty years earlier when he first shared his struggle with me. Like others I've mentioned in this book, he mistook just the "telling" of his secret as something redemptive. I had often wondered what had become of Tom. I read his e-mail initially with sadness because of what it had ended up costing him—his health, his career, and his reputation. Unfortunately, I see this happen increasingly in the lives of our leaders.

I've spoken with Tom a few times since he wrote. I wanted to find out more about his life now, after he'd gotten rid of the persona he had constructed to hide it all. I encountered a man who is more broken in a good way, much more authentic, with a new grasp and appreciation of grace. He'll tell you that it was the rediscovery of grace for him, personally and in community, that made the difference. Tom had finally begun, with the help of other men, to learn how God meets our corruptions with his grace. This is a crucial principle we all need to understand better. It's the normal work of God in his people.

"HEROES" OF FAITH

Not long ago I was reading Hebrews 11, the chapter about all the heroes and heroines of the faith. Sixteen specific individuals are mentioned, as well as several groups of people, all now encompassing the "cloud of witnesses" who lived by faith (Hebrews 12:1). As I read this list, several people jumped out at me. David was one. Yes, we know he was a man "after God's own heart," jealous for God's reputation and for Israel. As a man sensitive to God's Spirit and leading, he was the author of many psalms. The life of David, displayed through the psalms he wrote and through the texts written about him, is, I once heard, the longest narrative of a human life in all of ancient literature. We're all aware of his heartfelt, gut-wrenching confession in Psalm 51, a standard for what it means to repent.

But all was not right with David. David could be a hothead, often leading with his emotions rather than his brain. He was often impetuous in responding to people and situations. He made mistakes, at times going ahead of God. From the books of 1 and 2 Samuel and

1 and 2 Kings we find that even in a man so passionate for God, things were not all right and good. For instance, we find that David had many wives and concubines, a situation that is always accompanied by complications in Scripture and that always caused trouble, and misery for both the men and the women involved. In short, what we see in the life of David is a redeemed man with lots of unredeemed stuff still in him.

Then I saw Samson, one of the judges of Israel, on this list in Hebrews 11 of those who lived "by faith." I remember thinking, *God, you've got to be kidding!* Samson was the bad boy of his day, the party animal who was always getting into trouble. If there had been tabloids in his day, he would have made many front covers! Early on, when he was still probably a youth, Samson saw a young Philistine woman with whom he became smitten. Boldly, he told his parents, "Now get her for me as my wife" (Judges 14:2). Remember, though, that God had strictly forbidden intermarriage between Israel and their foreign neighbors. He knew that these people would lead Israel into idol worship. However, Samson simply didn't care. His parents tried to put up a fight about this, saying, "Is there not a woman among the daughters of your relatives, or among all our people, that you must go to take a wife from the uncircumcised Philistines?" Samson replied, "Get her for me, for she is right in my eyes" (Judges 14:2–3). Unfortunately, Samson's parents lacked the courage to resist Samson despite the damage they probably knew his choice would bring. They gave in to his desires.

Judges also tells us that Samson had a habit of visiting prostitutes (16:1–3). We observe Samson's unabated sexual appetite most vividly in his desire for Delilah. His relationship with her nearly caused Israel's downfall; it was, however, the cause of his own disgrace and death. It can't be denied that much of Samson's life was not governed by his head or heart, but by the lower half of his body!

So how could Samson be singled out as a hero, a man "of faith" that we're to emulate? Seems odd, but if you do biblical research on many of the people listed in Hebrews 11, you'll find very broken people with lots of character flaws—people who made horrendous mistakes and sinned greatly. How is it that the writer can commend even these people to us? It's a dramatic example of how God blesses people like this (actually, like us!), because he gives his grace to us even when we are still covered with our corruptions, and he does this as a rule, not an exception. God absolutely takes our sin seriously, but God still works his grace in and through our sinful lives. It's a typical picture of the average follower of Christ. And most of those listed here were spiritual leaders of one type or another!

Who do you look to as spiritual leaders? Many look to the Puritans, even though they often get a bad rap. The fact is, though, that the Puritans knew more about the human heart than you probably realize. One leader, Thomas Watson, wrote in 1666 about the way God works in fallen people, even in their vices and sleaze. Listen to what he has to say:

> Often in the godly, a little grace is mixed with much corruption. . . . There are, in the best of saints, interweavings of sin and grace: a dark side with the light; much pride mixed with humility; much earthliness mixed with heavenliness. . . . In many of the regenerate there is more corruption than grace. So much smoke that you can scarcely discern any fire; so much distrust that you can hardly see any faith. . . . A Christian in this life is like a glass that has more froth than wine.[35]

This certainly helps us understand how some of the folks listed in Hebrews 11 made it there. It wasn't by their effort or strict rule keeping. No, it was a work of God's Spirit in them, in the midst of their polluted hearts. Watson continues: "But though grace lives with so much difficulty, like the infant that struggles for breath, yet being born of God, it is immortal. Grace conflicting with corruptions is like a ship tossed and beaten by the waves, yet it weathers the storm and at last gets to the desired haven."[36]

Do you see what this all means? When we're at our worst, with no strength to keep on fighting our corrupt nature and the sins that plague us, God's grace is bigger than our ability to fail and fall. Grace is hidden in and through all our corruptions—if we belong to Christ, if we're his. Watson wonderfully captures this theme when he states, "As fire may be hidden in the embers, so grace may be hidden under many disorders of the soul."[37] Not only should that give us a new, realistic perspective, it should give us more patience and care for those who may take three steps forward and one backward now and then in their struggle against sin.

What hope this is! I think it's marvelous how Watson uses the example of a fire. People in 1666 would have known about fires. They were necessary for survival. Open fires were used to cook every meal and to ward off the damp and cold. To liken God's grace to something hidden in the embers of a dying fire dramatically emphasizes a truth Watson wanted people to be reminded of several times a day: we belong to a God who thinks of ingenious ways to remind us of great biblical truths! Consider circumcision, the sign of the covenant indicating that Israel was set apart and called to be holy as God's adopted people. God had the households of Israel perform circumcision on each male born into the family. Jesus himself underwent circumcision as part of Jewish law.

What an imaginative illustration of God's ownership, one by which *all* men would be reminded of the covenant several times a day! Each time a male among God's people urinated, he would be reminded of who he was and of God's saving grace. Now that's creative, to say the least! It was a vivid reminder that God's people needed to be rescued from themselves, and we still need to be reminded of that. In your dealings with your own heart and sexual struggles, you need to remind yourself that you have been, are being, and still need to be saved, and this is the work of the gospel in you.

William Law was a pastor in the Church of England in the mid-1700s who was kicked out of the church when he could no longer pledge allegiance to the king. Although you've probably not heard of him, I'll bet you've heard of two of his star pupils, John and Charles Wesley. They influence believers through their teachings and their music to this day. In 1761, just a few months before his death, Law wrote a long sermon to a group of pastors entitled, *An Humble, Earnest and Affectionate Address to the Clergy*. Law urged these men, "That our salvation consists wholly in being saved from *ourselves,* or that which we are by Nature."[38] He went on to explain how the gospel was summed up in this one idea: our ongoing need to be saved from ourselves, from those places that our hearts, when left to themselves, naturally take us. A growing Christian is one who is aware both of his struggle against sin and his ongoing need to be rescued from himself, from the base and debilitating desires of his fallen heart.

In your struggle against sin, don't you often feel the weight of your corruptions? Of course you do. Just feeling that weight, especially if you are isolated, living out of your own head, can take you more deeply into despair and sin if you let it. You need to see, though, that the gospel is for the corrupt. Who are the corrupt? Those who feel like they're a fraud, a sham, a hoax, a wannabe. Yes, the gospel is for those who feel they are always on the outside, never quite making it in; those who are aware that, by background and nature, they really don't belong.

In my late teens, before I became a Christian, I often felt like a wannabe, never quite making it, always on the outside looking in. Then, as I began to read Scripture, I encountered a Jesus who totally disrupted me. Here was a man who claimed to be God yet whose ministry centered on the moral rejects of society. Intentionally and compassionately, he set his time, attention, and affection on the moral outcasts. He was always pursuing those you wouldn't want on your ball team or anywhere else! One day it hit me. I was one of the people Jesus would have wanted to spend time with. This realization began to totally disrupt my life.

If you struggle sexually, this is where you live on any given day. You know you're on the outside looking in, and you live your life afraid that someone will find out that you're a fraud. But the amazing news of the gospel is that someone *has* found you out and he offers his forgiveness and grace to you anyway, just where you are, again and again. How does that make you feel? Why wouldn't you want to believe it? What gets in the way? You need to let this truth really sink deep down, from your head into your heart. Does knowing that you have a loving heavenly Father like this result in any kind of joy? It should.

Pastor Tim Keller describes in one of his sermons how our idols can be made less powerful and influential. He explains that we are either sowing to the flesh or to the Spirit at any given time in our lives (Galatians 6:8). "We sow to the Spirit," he says, "when we obey God out of a grateful joy that comes from a deep awareness of our status as children of God."[39] The problem is that I don't know many men who struggle intensely with sex who know much about this kind of joy! Joy is a foreign concept to most who deal with relentless sexual temptations. Your joy may have died long ago. But did you get the essence of this? We can be empowered to obedience, but it doesn't come from mustering up our resolve or pulling ourselves up by our bootstraps. Rather, it comes from a grateful joy. And where does *that* come from? It comes from a deep awareness of our status as God's children. This awareness of belonging to a loving God is a strange concept to many. Maybe you had it at one time, but your scarred heart and checkered history have obscured it. Any hint of joy has become masked, shrouded, and buried by your guilt and shame. You rarely see yourself in these terms anymore. If anything, you think of yourself as the black sheep in God's family.

One of the most destructive consequences of our sin is that it takes away our hope of ever being different. We keep thinking that if we can just stop doing what we're doing, things will be okay. But most of us can't stop. And just stopping would leave a vacuum that would feel strange and unfamiliar. Where would our hearts turn then, since they always will want to turn to something other than God? Whenever we try to curtail a bad habit, there will always be a feeling of dread and loss. Something else must fill the gap, something that will transform both heart and behavior. That something must be Christ.

THE EXPULSIVE POWER OF A NEW AFFECTION

In the early 1800s Scottish pastor Thomas Chalmers wrote a sermon entitled, "The Expulsive Power of a New Affection." It's a very long sermon, but Tim Keller does a good job summarizing the point that Chalmers makes. He puts it like this:

> Seldom do any of our habits or flaws disappear by a process of extinction or by the force of mental determination. But what cannot be normally destroyed may be dispossessed; the only way to dispossess the heart of an old affection is by the expulsive power of a new one. . . . The heart's desire for one particular object may be conquered, but its desire to have some object of absolute love is unconquerable. It is only when admitted into the number of God's children through faith in Jesus Christ that the spirit of adoption is poured out on us; it is then and only then, that the heart, brought under the mastery of one great predominant affection, is delivered from the tyranny of all its former desires, and the only way that deliverance is possible.[40]

Let's apply this to the struggles most guys have with pornography and other sexual sin. We seem to spend an amazing amount of time trying to avoid, destroy, or kill the thing that gets us in trouble. I mean, what happens after you go through a bad bout of lust that entails some acting out (i.e., viewing porn, masturbation, etc.)? Most guys I know refocus their attention, strategize, redouble their efforts, recommit to some kind of renewed vow or plan and, eventually, rebound somewhat. As good as these efforts seem to be, they still entail nothing but a lot of self-effort. Your efforts at getting back on track are all done without anyone knowing where your major battles lie. Isn't that how many of you attempt to regain your footing? Sure it is.

I am in no way minimizing the importance of one's need to recommit himself to a holy and chaste life and to do whatever it takes to ensure we actually live that way. This effort is, however, made even more complex by the fact that the continued misuse of sex, especially pornography, also has damaging physiological, psychological, and addictive side effects. Most of what I've covered in this book is about sin's impact on the soul. But we need to remember that our soul does not exist in a vacuum. The soul is housed in a physical body, a body that is impacted by our thinking and our behavior.

Increasingly, medical and psychological studies are addressing the detrimental impact that porn has on the body, especially the brain, in cases of long-term, continued use. Psychiatrist Norman Doidge, author of *The Brain That Changes Itself*, points to the fact that our brains are neuroplastic; that is, they undergo actual structural change with repetitive exposure to stimuli, especially pornography. Viewing pornography triggers the brain's reward center, which releases a powerful chemical called dopamine, giving us a special thrill or sense of euphoria. Doidge reports that the reward centers themselves are altered. When that happens, people will compulsively seek out behaviors that continue to trigger the dopamine discharge.[41] In other words, there is a physiologically addictive aspect to a struggle with pornography. He argues that the altered reward center and damaged dopamine system cause one to become increasingly tolerant of sexual stimuli, resulting in the craving for more in order to get the same rush. That's why masturbation almost always accompanies the pornography since the desired end result is the powerful feelings of orgasm.

Doesn't this help explain why dealing with sexual temptations seems to be such a laborious and often self-defeating endeavor? So much seems to work against getting and staying free from it all. Can someone who has spent years in these life-crippling behaviors ever live as if he hadn't done so? Probably not. This doesn't mean, however, that change isn't possible. You *can* deal successfully with your struggles and receive significant ongoing healing in this area. It just means that your heart (and brain) will not "forget" what you once ran to for relief and refuge (your sexual sin). This means you need to remain vigilant about the state of your heart at all times because you remain vulnerable in these areas of your life. In recognizing this vulnerability, you are also finally able to see that you will always be dependent on God's grace. And this is a good thing! The bottom line is this: while the gospel isn't magical, it *is* powerful and effective to change the heart. This can lead to a change in our thinking and behavior.

In light of the powerfully destructive forces that often unite to keep us in physical and spiritual bondage, Chalmers's message about the heart is still extremely important. We must attend to the effects of sin on our body and on our soul. Chalmers's point was that it's the stuff of the heart (the bad affections) that gets us into trouble, but those bad affections *can* be dispossessed. What does that mean? *Dispossessed* is a word we don't use much these days. It means to be stripped or divested of something. It means that something loses its power. It ceases to have the pull, attraction, allure, charm, and beauty to lead us into sin the way it once did. Chalmers said that this can't be accomplished though fortitude, stamina, or resolve. Something must replace the bad affections!

This is where I have some trouble with the recovery movement. I know that a lot of good things happen in recovery groups as people experience change in their behaviors. Nevertheless, I don't like the word "recovery." I don't think it's a very biblical concept. It falls too far short. I like to think instead in terms of "biblical change" which depends on discovery (rather than recovery) and is therefore more hopeful. One might say that recovery is the side effect of discovery. I need to discover what God has done for me in Christ and how the gospel beckons me to him when I feel least worthy or capable of moving towards God. My heart longs to discover that he still cares for me no matter how I have disregarded him. It's the discovery of God's heart for the brokenhearted and crushed in spirit that is the most powerful realization! That's why "recovery," the idea of stopping something to get back to a time before I had the problem, falls short of true biblical transformation. As believers, we must begin to live out of something else, some other type of life-force. Most self-help programs refer to that something else as a "higher power." I'm thankful that some Christian groups using the recovery model have correctly identified that power as coming entirely and solely from Christ.

Martyn Lloyd-Jones said that living the Christian life is always a combination of God's power and our activity. It's not one or the other. It's both! Faith is not passive. It's very active. It engages with reality and enables action. This prayer from *The Valley of Vision* captures it precisely.

When thy Son, Jesus, came into my soul instead of sin,
    he became more dear to me than sin had formerly had been;
    his kindly rule replaced sin's tyranny.
Teach me to believe that if ever I would have any sin subdued
    I must not only labor to overcome it,
    but must invite Christ to abide in the place of it,
    and he must become to me more than vile lust had been;
    that his sweetness, power, life, may be there.
Thus I must seek a grace from him contrary to sin,
    but must not claim it apart from himself.[42]

There you have it! My question to you is, just how is Christ becoming dearer to you than your sin? Are you allowing *his* sweetness, power, and life to impact your heart, even in the midst of your struggles? Are you turning your thoughts to God, letting his view of you trump the turbulence of your heart as you struggle with temptation? This is how his grace is found. Will you seek it?

Are you willing to come out of the spell you've been under in your struggles? Maybe it's the spell of believing that your sin still has something life-giving for you. Maybe it's the spell of your hopelessness that anything will ever change in your life. Maybe it's the spell of a pornified-heart, which looks at everything and everyone through sexualized lenses. Or maybe it's the spell made all the more powerful by your commitment to continue trying to handle it all on your own.

C. S. Lewis gives a great example of how intoxicating this kind of deception can be in his book *The Silver Chair*. The three main characters in this story find themselves in the domain of the Lady of the Green Kirtle who is, in reality, the evil queen of the underworld. At one point, Eustace, Jill, and Puddleglum find themselves captive deep below ground. They find a knight clad in black and bound in chains to a silver chair. He had been taken captive years ago by the queen when she killed his mother. This knight doesn't know that he is the Prince Rilian for whom Eustace and Jill have been searching.

At one point, the queen enters the room and discovers that Prince Rilian has been freed and the chair destroyed. She begins to question all four of them. As they begin to talk about the world beyond the underworld—the world they know exists—the queen attempts to lull their senses to sleep. She attempts to inhibit their ability to recall the truth about that other world by conjuring a mist or green fog that begins to enfold each of the four as they speak to the queen.

Enveloped in this fog, each attempts to recall a point of truth and is met with challenges from the queen. Prince Rilian, now beginning to see a little more clearly, brings up the land of Narnia. The queen responds that there is no such place as Narnia. It's a fantasy world; there is no other world than hers. Then someone mentions the sky. She responds that there is no sky. Another brings up the sun. She says that there is no such thing as a sun. Someone brings up Aslan. She disavows his existence too. Each time she speaks, the mist flows around the four people, forcing them to repeat what she says. At that moment, they are totally under her spell and power.

Perhaps you have experienced something like this in your own life. Does this scene mirror the way you feel when you are overwhelmed by your weak, polluted, and crushed heart? These days I find more and more men walking around as prisoners of their own sexual fog. One man recently explained to me that he knew something was dreadfully wrong as he began to lose track of whole blocks of time, spending entire days in a stupor brought on by his sexual fantasies and time in front of his computer. He had also fallen into a deep depression.

In the scene from Lewis's book, something else interesting happens. As the mist envelops them, overwhelming their wills and distorting their senses, Puddleglum rushes forward and stamps his feet on the fire the queen had lit in the fireplace. When he does this, the green fog vanishes instantly. Puddleglum tells the queen that she can never make them forget the truth and now she must show them the way out of the darkness of that underworld cave. How does one get that kind of courage? Let's talk about that in the next chapter.

FOR REFLECTION AND DISCUSSION

1. Sampson's life was motivated by impulsivity—seeking his pleasure now. In what ways do you do that in your life? Does John's explanation of Samson discourage you or encourage you?

2. How does it strike you to find out that you will always need to be rescued from yourself—and from those dark places you're tempted to go to for life?

3. In what ways can you begin to apply the truth that, in order to overcome any sin, Christ must become "more dear" to you than your lusts and sin?

Chapter 9

Walking Out of the Fog and into the Light

Of all the people I've been involved with through the years, no one sticks out in my mind more vividly than Jack. His story will be etched in my heart as long as I live.

Jack had come to realize that he was attracted to other men as a teenager. Around the age of twenty, in the early 1960s, he came to Christ through the witness of a Bible college student who was sharing his faith on the streets of Philadelphia. Residing in center city Philly, Jack began attending Tenth Presbyterian Church.

Back then churches didn't seek to address the needs of those struggling with same-sex attractions. After several years, disillusioned and unable to reconcile his faith and his feelings, Jack left the church and settled down in a gay relationship for the next fifteen years. Even though he was deeply entrenched in the gay subculture of Philadelphia with its parties and clubs and was in a single relationship, Jack was wrestling internally the entire time. In the mid-eighties, as a forty-four-year-old, Jack discovered Harvest USA through one of the ads I described earlier in this book, aimed at reaching those who were disenfranchised from the church but still questioning.

Although Jack was in a committed homosexual relationship, in our one-on-one conversations, we saw that he was genuinely searching, hungry for truth, so he was invited into our Bible study/support group. We took a "wait and see what happens" attitude. One thing I certainly knew: Like many men who end up in one of our groups, there was absolutely no human reason for his being there. But it was obvious that, as we shared more of the love of Christ and the grace of the gospel, and talked about faith and repentance to the men in that group, something inside Jack was churned up.

About three months after Jack began attending our little group (which Tenth Church had begun), I was walking to my office in one of the immense, brownstone twin houses that Philly is famous for. As I approached my door on Spruce Street that morning, I noticed a pile of furniture and boxes on the sidewalk next to my door. Now, people were moving in and out of buildings all the time on my block, so at first I thought nothing of it. Then, as I approached the pile of stuff, I saw a note with my name on it. It said simply, "John, I believe what you're saying. Jack."

I was blown away! Later that day, I found out that Jack had become convicted overnight that the gospel was really true. He realized in a God-given moment of insight that he was looking for life and nourishment in his gay relationship (and with men in general) that only God could provide. Convinced that he had to flee, he did— at the exact moment of spiritual breakthrough! He gathered up his personal belongings, all that he owned in the world, and deposited them on the doorstep of our building, the place he had come to see as his haven of safety and acceptance.

We had a really good problem on our hands. Jack needed a place to live. We got him a room in a household of Christian men from Tenth. Leaving behind the social and relational network and camaraderie of the gay community meant he had no friends to associate with. We became those friends—as did, more importantly, the folks at Tenth Church, where Jack resumed attending.

Over the next months and years, Jack's life became a display of quiet but determined grace as he grew in Christ and became more verbal about his testimony, giving it on more than one occasion from the pulpit at Tenth. Jack became a very active, vocal, and beloved member of the church, serving in some of the cutting-edge ministries for which Tenth is known. His story was very much one of process, as he put one foot in front of the other, following Christ and making the daily decision that God's ways were better than his own. All that happened in his life and in the lives of others through him was the fruit of a renewed faith and the life of repentance that Jack experienced.

As I recall Jack's life, it still stirs me. Jack is no longer with us. He had a heart attack several years ago and is now with the Lord.[43] But let me tell you why I shared his story. Jack's initial steps toward Christ in the midst of his sexual mess are a wonderful example of what faith is about—how it spurs us to action in spite of our fears, our apparent powerlessness, and ourselves.

What happened to Jack is similar to what happened when Puddle-glum suddenly put out the queen's fire and demanded that she show them the way out of the underworld. This is the essence of faith. In the Bible, faith is never a passive thing. It is active and action-oriented. Faith, or belief, has to move from head to heart to action. If it does not lead to action, it's usually not true biblical faith. Let me give you an example. Let's say you were sitting in your chair watching television. You suddenly think you smell smoke. You get up, look around and go toward the source of the smell to see if it's real and if you're in any imminent danger. As you approach the door to your kitchen, you actually see flames through a small window. The smell of smoke is even stronger, and you actually feel heat radiating from the other side of the door. Do you just go back to your chair and resume watching television? Well, if you do, you must not really believe that there is a fire about to burn your house down!

The same is true as you deal with your sexual struggles while trying to live in faith, repentance, and obedience. Recognizing the dire state of things and actually believing that you're in danger will only be evidenced by the action steps you take to confront it. What steps are you willing to take, however scary and uncomfortable, to help you dispel the sexual fog you've been walking in—perhaps for years? Whenever we begin to take steps, even baby steps, to deal with our lives and hearts, God honors it. One way he does that is to help us see the "thing"—whatever our hearts mistakenly and sinfully depend on—more clearly as we decide to tackle it.

UNDERSTANDING YOUR OWN HEART'S DESIRES

In *Mere Christianity*, C. S. Lewis talks about society's view of sexual repression, a hot topic in the psychological community even back in 1943. Lewis's argument is as fresh and relevant now as it was when he first wrote it. Even today in some academic and scientific circles, you will hear of the danger of trying to hold back sexual desire or to put restrictions on it. Those in the secular mental health field will often say that to inhibit sexual expression is risky. But in his chapter on sexual morality, Lewis addresses this concern by pointing out the difference between *repressing* desires (bottling them up) and *suppressing* them (resisting them). "On the contrary, those who are seriously attempting chastity are more conscious, and soon know a great deal more about their own sexuality than anyone else. They come to know their desires as Wellington knew Napoleon, or as Sherlock Holmes knew Moriarty."[44]

Lewis's point is important. When people wrestle positively with reining in their sexual desires, when they even attempt to live the way God wants them to, they are not trying to *repress* anything. On the contrary, those who want to get honest with God about all this can begin to engage the process with everything in them. The new goals of holiness and chastity cause them to know and understand their hearts in a totally different light.

I really like Lewis's examples of Wellington and Napoleon, Sherlock Holmes and Moriarty. The people in each pair were archenemies, and as such, they studied each other's tactics and strategies backwards and forwards. They intimately understood the inner workings of the one they had to fight! They became experts at understanding what's there, just as a ratcatcher comes to know rats and a plumber comes to know the workings of leaky pipes. Lewis describes those who are trying to walk in chastity as those who are learning a great deal more about their desires and hearts in the process. Our intentional striving to holiness actually leads us to know more of the essence of our desires and sinful hearts than those who are indifferent or never enter the fray! Lewis says that even attempting this will bring light, but to continue to indulge will result in an ongoing fog.

Maybe you understand what Lewis is saying here. But I would guess that you and most of the men in your life know nothing of this kind of heart awareness. The benefit of understanding what is going on in our hearts is that it enables us to know how the gospel needs to be applied to the areas that surface as we come to know ourselves.

In a university graduate course in Christian counseling, I always taught my students something that drove them up the wall. I would teach them *not* to lead their counselees into repentance too quickly! Inevitably, this would be met with stunned expressions and exclamations of, "What! That's why we're there as counselors, isn't it? That's the goal, right?" To which I'd answer, "Yes . . . maybe, in time."

I would go on to explain that those caught in sin, especially sexual sin, need to know more of the essence of what they're dealing with and why they are continually falling for the lies it promises. They need to know exactly what they are repenting of. Counseling, and even repentance, can fall prey to the false goal of simply hunting for the surface issue or problem—that keyboard, that gentlemen's club, that chat-line, that personal sexual habit. And let's admit it: it's often much easier to get someone to repent of things like this—just "stop" something, just avoid or quit doing that "thing"—than it is to deal with the mess of the heart. Yet Jesus said that it's out of the heart that all the troublesome stuff comes because the heart is the true source of the trouble.

Anyone who attempts to apply the gospel to what they find internally soon learns that the heart is a messy thing—and men hate mess! As a result, you may not want to know what's there or how to deal with it. But as Lewis said, there is light in resisting sin and in attempting virtue. And that light is meant to shine in on the mess. We need to know the stuff that stinks about our hearts. Getting at this dark stuff is what the gospel is all about.

What gives us the courage to attack our warped desires? It's what gave Puddleglum the boldness to rush at the underworld queen. It's what gave my friend Jack the strength to take drastic, life-saving steps. You've got to see that, though your heart is fickle, God's hold on you can give you that courage. Believing and resting in God's love for you in Christ is what lets you know, somewhere, somehow, deep inside, that it will be okay to wade into it all. In so doing, being convinced that God offers us more, we can face our fears because we know we will find God waiting for us. Scotty Smith puts it this way in a prayer that reflects on the story of the Prodigal Son:

> So, Father, as I come to you today, I take great comfort in knowing I'll *always* find you filled with compassion for me, even when my feelings are not fully engaged with you. As I saunter toward

you, you're always running toward me in Jesus. As I'm glad to see you, you see me from afar and are *thrilled* at the sighting. . . . You don't just put your hand on my shoulder; you throw your arms around me in the gospel. And though my affection for you wavers, you will shower me with multiple kisses all day long, for you love your children with an everlasting, unwavering love. . . . It's not my grasp of you but your grasp of me in the gospel that matters most. It's not the enjoyment of my peace with you but the assurance that you are at peace with me, this is the anchor for my soul.[45]

What he's saying here echoes what Thomas Chalmers said about the expulsive power of a new affection. When we begin to see *God's affection for us,* it changes us radically. In Tim Keller's paraphrase of what Chalmers said, he concluded: "There is only one way that the root of your personality can be changed and that is by an experience of love. Only when your heart experiences love from a new source beyond anything it has ever known before will our heart start to move toward that source. It'll start to be deeply changed, and that is the only way. Then it will be reforged; then it will be changed, at the deepest level. It's the only way."[46]

Did you get that last part? The deep change that needs to take place in your soul is not anything you do. It's not about good intentions or twelve steps to take or checking off a list of action steps. That's not how you change, really change, deeply change. What matters most is the radical awareness that you're totally accepted and loved by the God who is at peace *with you.* If you have even a glimpse of what this is all about, don't hesitate. Realize that he will be with you as you pursue help for your neglected heart. Be aware that self-protection and fear will be right there too, attempting to sabotage any steps you take to bring light to your soul, sexually speaking.

Walking out of your fog into the light must be your choice, though. No one can make you do it or talk you into it. At this point, you may still be like the man who said to Jesus, "I believe; help my unbelief," struggling between action and inaction. You've got to believe that God has something much better for you and that, in Christ, all things are possible. Go for it! Run to Christ, grasping at whatever level of belief you have in the love with which he has taken ahold of you. As Jesus said to that man, "All things are possible for one who believes" (Mark 9:23).

FOR REFLECTION AND DISCUSSION

1. How do you understand the difference between repressing vs. resisting sexual desires? When you find success in resisting your temptations, do you find yourself understanding a bit more of your heart and what is driving it? Explain.

2. The story about Jack showed how much he took the gospel seriously, by taking steps to leave his old life behind even when he had no game plan going forward. What would you need to do in order to do that in your life?

3. If you are still not willing to take a step forward, then reflect on what you are still getting out of your sexual sin; what you think God might not be giving you? Can you face that squarely and talk to God honestly about it?

Chapter 10

Okay, What Do I Do Now?

The city of Florence is home to Michelangelo's famous statue of David. When Michelangelo was commissioned to create this statue, how do you think he prepared for the task, knowing that his next commission would likely depend on the success of this one? I imagine that he would begin by finding the right tools for the job. Only the best hammers or chisels would do. I have three grown children who are all artists of one type or another. Every time one of them needed a new tool for an assignment, we'd make a trip to Utrecht's, the premier art supply store in center city Philadelphia. No matter what they needed, it always seemed like it was a $100 purchase at least.

Once Michelangelo assembled his tools, I would imagine that he began the search for the perfect piece of stone. It might be granite or marble, but again, only the best would do. His artistic vision, his reputation, and his livelihood depended on it.

But here is how Michelangelo actually began his search for what became one of his most famous statues. Walking through a junkyard of discarded and previously used marble, he saw an enormous piece of stone. It had been left out in the elements for forty years, a damaged, hand-me-down piece of marble that had been worked on by a prior sculptor.

Perhaps it had been deemed too flawed, with too many cracks and defects. But as Michelangelo stood there, looking intently at that imperfect piece of stone, imagining what it could become in his master craftsman hands, Michelangelo found his David. He got it to his studio and . . . well, you know the rest of the story.

Isn't that the way it is in your life and mine? God takes the broken and damaged parts of our hearts, lives, and desires and makes us works of art with his own master craftsman hands. He takes the parts of our story that bring us the most shame—the things we'd die if anyone knew—and makes them (and us) things of beauty. That is Christ in us, the hope of glory (Colossians 1:27)! Can you dare to believe that he wants to do this in your life, in your struggles with temptation and sin?

I hope you haven't skipped to read this chapter first! If you're like most guys, you'd rather have ten steps of concrete things to do than think about everything I've talked about in this book. We'd rather work a formula than submit to a process that will be scary and unknown, even if it will ultimately change our hearts and character. So don't give in to the temptation to just "do" something else, to come up with a new plan, a retooled strategy, alone—again. There are no shortcuts to believing the difficult but life-giving, heart-changing, and joy-enhancing truths I've shared in these chapters.

What I hope this book has done is to move your heart to a new openness to seek the help you know you need. So the major "doing" aspect of all this is the commitment to do something—or to do something again—about your heart and your sexual struggles. Here are a few steps you can take to get started, if you believe at least a little of what I've been talking about.

THE FIRST STEP TO TAKE: REACH OUT TO ONE PERSON

If you are a guy, whether single or married, who has never opened up to another person about your struggles with sex, find someone you trust from your church or other Christian men's community and share with him what's going on. Maybe you talked with someone in the past but now, years later, due to a new job, a new location, a new set of relationships, or just a commitment to self-protection and isolation, you need to do that again. When I tell men I've been discipling that they must tell another guy, inevitably they will say, "I don't know who I could trust."

I tell them to think of guys, even one guy, who has a solid, gospel-centered heart, who understands the reality of the struggle with sin. Maybe you've never heard him talk specifically about sexual issues, but from what you know of him in other contexts—through things he's said, things he's prayed—you sense he'd be someone you could talk with. Is there anyone you dare trust like this?

Maybe it's someone in a men's group you are already attending. Maybe it's your pastor, or maybe not. If you're thinking "not," know why. Is it just your fear of being exposed or "found out" by the head guy? Or is it that he really isn't trustworthy or approachable about these things, based on what you know of him? Ask God to help you as you think and pray about who this could be. Then, once that person is confirmed in your mind and heart, ask God for the power to follow through.

After your first few meetings with this man, as you've unpacked your story and your heart, ask him to help you come up with a care plan. This plan needs to incorporate the elements I've talked about in this book—what steps will be necessary for you to come out of the shadows, dealing honestly and authentically, with what has held you prisoner.

THE SECOND STEP: FIND SUPPORT IN COMMUNITY

As you take those first steps forward, remember the most basic first step for real change: You can't do this alone, and you need other men to walk with you. So you will need to join or form a small group of men who are wrestling with their own sexually fallen hearts.

These days, I find myself challenging men about where their "points of light" are throughout the week. Who are the men in your life who know you and your struggles? Sex is a bigger thing than we were ever meant to handle alone. Only when we allow the community of Christ (yes, selectively and not indiscriminately) in on our stuff will we set the stage to walk in freedom. I don't know many men who have had years of soul-neglect and, therefore, self-deception in this area, who can walk this road alone. We weren't meant to, and trying to has probably intensified your problems and damaged your spirit.

What are "points of light"? They are those places where you're known and where the means of grace (God's Word, fellowship, prayer, and worship) are a regular part of your time in the company of others. Everything about you might not be known by everyone—that is, every sordid detail of your situation and sexual history. But the facts are known by somebody. Some will know them in great detail, while others will have far less detail.

Do you see how important it is that you begin to allow some people to know you? If you can't find that first man to come clean with (not because you are afraid of doing it, but because you simply don't have anyone like that in your sphere of relationships), contact a Christian counselor and talk to him. A good counselor will also help you develop a care plan for yourself.

In addition, find out if your church has a group for men seeking to apply the gospel to pursue a holy life in this area. If your church doesn't have one, make a few calls or check online to see if other local churches sponsor such a group. Ask God for the courage to make that first contact, send that first e-mail, or make that call for help. This can often be the most difficult step. But you can do it through the power of the Holy Spirit. To borrow that Nike phrase from a few years back, "Just Do It!"

Getting involved in a biblical support group for sexual strugglers will be one of the hardest, but one of the most liberating steps you will take. Many men flinch at this step and retreat. One man I know sat outside in his car while the meeting he was intending on joining was taking place inside a building across the street. He was terrified at seeing someone he knew in that group. He was afraid of being known, reluctant to have his reputation diminished because now people would know something about him he had deceitfully kept hidden. It seemed like an eternity while he sat in the front seat of his car. Finally, following a short burst of desperate prayer, he swung open the door and walked inside. At the end of the group meeting, after he had finally confessed his struggle, and heard the confession of the other men in the group, he went home feeling liberated. Free. Hopeful. New.

The group meeting will be central to your healing and growth, but don't stop here. Someone committed to being in the light needs multiple places to go to ensure he is taking care of his heart well. The men who are involved at Harvest USA may attend one of our support accountability groups, attend their church's weekly men's group, and go to a smaller, more confidential discipleship group of three or four guys from their church. They may have a prayer partner with whom they meet weekly. Maybe they are trying to deal with the more personal nitty-gritty issues in private counseling. Then, of course, there's that important corporate point of light, our public worship of God with the body of Christ at church.

But don't be put off by all these meetings! Start small, but recognize that as you grow you'll see more value in growing with others in the body of Christ. That is, after all, what the church is for. God's work is primarily done in us, through others.

The common denominator in all of your small group points of light, whatever they may be, is that these are places you come out of your secret self. You end the hiding. All people don't have to know all things about you, but they do have to know where you struggle—the specific areas of life for which you are seeking the healing balm of the gospel. Yes, that means that the members of each group need to know something of your sexual struggles. They need to know enough (and some more than others) so that if all the men in these groups got together, they would have a similar and accurate picture of you. They would all know some of the major themes of your heart, and where you struggle to believe the gospel in light of your sexual temptations and history.

Does all this make sense? I certainly hope so. Your points of light are people whose mouths wouldn't drop open if someone asked, "Oh, did you know he struggles with _____?" That news wouldn't come as a shock.

Now, I admit that seeking out this kind of redemptive network is not common and it is certainly not natural! What's natural is to just keep going like you are, committed to your secret life, your secret sin, your secret everything! I'm talking about something quite *super*natural. You aren't the orchestrator or architect, although admittedly, you do have to *do* it! It's the perfect blending of *God's power* (convicting you and motivating you to do something) and *your activity* (you actually doing it). Men who pursue this kind of radical heart-and soul-care know there's something of God in the doing of the details. But, again, please realize that as much as you may know you need to do this, your own history and fallen heart will work against you. One of our staff, Tim Geiger, puts it this way:

> Those who struggle with patterns of sexual sin and brokenness have often been especially traumatized by relational disappointment—with parents, with caregivers, with peers or with others

who have been in authority over them at one time or another. As a result, they tend to especially shelter themselves from the risk of further harm and disappointment by doing two things: First, they distance themselves from others to create a protective relational buffer. Second, they continue to pursue a sense of intimacy, what we and others often call "false intimacy," through sexual sin.[47]

I like the way Tim points out this tendency in strugglers even as they attempt positive steps toward sexual wholeness. The temptation to hide from others and to escape the disappointments and difficulties of life by running headlong into sin is important to remember. For some of us, it remains an ongoing temptation that we must fight. Perhaps you are a little further along in dealing with all this in a healthy way. You are already doing something. Perhaps you have some sort of "accountability" or you are in an actual accountability group. My sincere congratulations for taking that bold step! Good for you—maybe. You see, it all depends on the essence of the group and what goes on there. Or, more pointedly, what's going on *in you* because of what's going on *in there*!

Unfortunately, I'm finding more and more accountability groups to be pretty ineffective. If people are not careful, these groups can become nothing more than places where people unload and confess but do not change. In many cases the confidentiality, safety, and security of such groups become the highest goal of the group, inhibiting group effectiveness. Now, of course, you need these elements in a group—that's a given. But when the dynamics of the group primarily center on the commonality of the struggle itself, then what can happen is that the expectation of change—and more importantly, how it happens—can get lost. Then the group will become ineffective and eventually collapse in a spirit of defeatism and hopelessness. Maybe you're in a group like this and know what I'm talking about.

Not long ago I was talking with a guy who had been in such a group for several years. He told me, "John, the problem is that no one in the group is experiencing any type of breakthrough or change." He went on to say that there is something of a "spiritual" basis to the group. A Scripture portion is read each week. Songs are sung. People share challenges, falls, and similar information. There's lots of camaraderie. But, he added, "The common denominator of why we're all there seems to be the problems themselves and the difficulty and shame of the struggles we share. This seems a more powerful glue to the group than does the hope and expectation that Christ will show up and actually do something." The expectancy that God would work in hearts to bring about new steps of faith and repentance had been "dumbed down," as had been the call to serious holiness. People in the group just weren't that hopeful that they would ever change.

This can happen so easily in a group. It's the natural path groups sometimes take if they turn inward and the essence of the group becomes the struggle itself. Ultimately, that's the wrong "content" to focus on so exclusively. The commonality and the camaraderie are important, but effective change groups must put the application of God's Word front and center. The Scriptures, carefully applied to real-life situations, must take priority and be highly valued as part of any group meeting. Otherwise, the group will remain comforting and safe but will lose its power to be an agent of change. Don't get me wrong. I'm a fan of groups. I believe in them. Part of our ministry's mission is to help churches begin partner ministries, and I've seen groups used powerfully in the lives of hundreds of people over the years. I would say that groups can be used of God in ways that individual counseling can't match. Something happens in groups that can become a very significant part of how Christ meets people in a new way, giving them the hope of the gospel, as well as being a tangible symbol of God's love and care expressed through the group members.

When the centrality of the gospel is at the heart of a group, then the other elements of the group can be made more effective. There are three life-changing activities that must take place as part of any successful biblical support group. The first crucial element is *accountability*. Accountability happens when I speak honestly about my temptation, my sin, and the condition of my heart with other Christian brothers. This requires ruthless honesty about the destructive stuff that fills and fuels my heart and speaking of it with other men. *Discipleship* is the second, *central* element, which I have already mentioned. As a group member, I am growing in faith and in God's truth and grasping more and more who I really am as God's child because of God's love for me. I can expect to see step-by-step movement (even if they are only small steps) and growth as I take hold of the reality of the gospel. Discipleship happens where I am and helps me apply the gospel to all the chaos, conflict, and confusion in my own heart, in order to make me a new and different person. Effective discipleship also enables me to get out of myself; to begin to love and serve others with my time, energy, and resources—because of what God is doing in me and what Christ is coming to mean to me. Third, there's the important element of *transparency*. Transparency is when I commit daily—with everyone, and not just with the members of my group—to living openly and without deceit, offering my life and the motives of my heart to the examination of others! Transparency may seem like accountability, but transparency is when I begin ruthlessly speaking the truth about everything I do, on a day-to-day basis. Because my sexual struggles and sin have been hidden for so long, I realize that lying and deceit have become a part of my daily habits. Now, by God's power, I learn to walk in the light and no longer in the darkness.

Do you see how the ordinary "accountability" group may fall far short of being an effective agent of change? That's because the element of accountability is only one of several things that are needed, and it's not even the most important one. But we often mistake it as such, omitting other crucial building blocks to wholeness.

I know that when it comes to that last ingredient, transparency, you may be thinking, *John, that seems like death! The accountability part is hard enough, but transparency, with everyone?* Believe me, it may seem like death, but it's the way to real life! It's the way to a clear conscience and to knowing God's love and acceptance through others who are on your team, rooting for you! There's nothing like it. If you've not experienced it, you may just have to take my word for it. Small groups and one-on-one-or-two-or-three connections like this are what have helped change my life for over forty years now. Having relationships like this, where I'm reminded of the gospel through others, is what's often made it possible for me to preach the gospel to myself in challenging situations, when my heart could easily head "south" into dark and destructive places.

Once you have found a group or started one of your own, there are a number of good resources to use. Our ministry uses a workbook that one of our staff members, David White, has written: *Sexual Sanity for Men: Re-Creating Your Mind in a Crazy Culture*. Written in a day-by-day, week-by-week devotional format, it is a great resource to dig into God's Word. As I said in the preface, there are now a number of resources you can find.[48] But remember, a resource is only a tool to get gospel truths deeper into your heart. The actual power for starting to live in a different way and to be a different person comes from sitting with Jesus. This needs to happen *regularly* in the presence of other men who know how much they need Jesus too. You need to do this for as long as it takes! For the average man who comes into one of our groups, that can be anywhere from two to three years. And even once you have (largely) dealt with your sexual struggles, this rhythm of coming to Jesus will form the basis of faith and obedience for the rest of your life and will keep you from falling back into the same old patterns.

Finally, I mentioned in chapter 1 the need for men to protect themselves from the relentless sexual temptation that comes from the Internet and how easily it is now piped to us via an assortment of devices we all have: home computers, laptops, mobile phones, tablets, Internet-connected TVs, and game consoles. I'm talking about the need to install filters and accountability software on all of these devices. Yes, all of them. Just as someone who has a problem with alcohol cannot hope to avoid drinking if he is constantly around liquor, so a sexual struggler cannot hope to resist temptation when everyday there is unhindered access to porn. It's just too much for the struggler; in fact, it's too much for all of us, as well! There's another reason for installing protective software on your devices.

Remember what I said in chapter 9 about how resisting temptation is the way to finally begin understanding what's going on in your heart? Well, you won't learn about how your heart operates if you are continually being bombarded with porn and succumbing to it. Installing porn filters and accountability filters on everything and anything you use that accesses the web is essential.[49] And the group can be a great place for men to help one another with this, especially with respect to being accountability partners. The men in the group will know all the ways one can find to access porn, and they can ask the hard questions and help you come to the point of agreeing that you need this protective software, and making sure they are always in operation.

A guy in one of our groups once likened his initial steps of walking out of his fog, coming into the light, and getting much-needed help to something out of C. S. Lewis's *The Lion, the Witch and the Wardrobe*. He said that beginning to embrace this new journey, though unusual and somewhat scary, was like riding on Aslan's back, holding on tightly to his mane as he flew, but being taken to new worlds he had never envisioned because God was behind it all!

This can be true of you too. May God bless you on your new journey!

FOR REFLECTION AND DISCUSSION

1. Have you ever shared your secret struggles with someone else? How did it go? What did it feel like? Was it helpful/not helpful? How?

2. What is the one thing you fear the most by talking to someone about your struggle? What are you most afraid of losing?

3. What are the things you would be gaining by getting all this out in the open? Can you begin to pray in this direction with God, believing that he has good things for you?

Endnotes

1. John Charles Ryle, *Knots Untied: Being Plain Statements on Disputed Points in Religion from the Standpoint of an Evangelical Churchman* (London: National Protestant Church Union, 1898), 417.

2. Paul David Tripp, *Sex & Money: Pleasures That Leave You Empty and Grace That Satisfies* (Wheaton, IL: Crossway, 2013), 88–89.

3. "Cyber-porn held responsible for increase in sex addiction," *Washington Times*, January 26, 2000, http://www.washingtontimes.com/news/2000/jan/26/20000126-010843-1665r/?page=all.

4. Patrick F. Fagan, "The Effects of Pornography on Individuals, Marriage, Family and Community," Marriage & Religious Inst., Family Research Council, Love & Responsibility Project: Center for Study of Catholic Higher Ed. *Scribd,* 11 Dec. 2009. http://www.scribd.com/doc/23930556/The-Effects-of-Pornography-on-Individuals-Marriage-Family-and-Community. I came across this statistic and this study through the Covenant Eyes Pornography Statistics published in February 2014.

5. "ChristiaNet Poll Finds that Evangelicals are Addicted to Porn," *Marketwired,* August 7, 2006, http://www.marketwired.com/press-release/christianet-poll-finds-that-evangelicals-are-addicted-to-porn-703951.htm.

6. Bob Sullivan, "Porn at Work Problem Persists," *Technology & Science/Security, MSNBC,* September 6, 2004, http://www.msnbc.msn.com/id/5899345/, As compiled by Covenant Eyes, http://www.covenanteyes.com/pornography-facts-and-statistics/, 2011.

7. Violet Blue, "Are more women OK with watching porn?" *CNN.com/Living,* July 24, 2009, http://www.cnn.com/2009/LIVING/personal/07/24/o.women.watching.porn/index.html.

8. Kimberly Giles, "Are Romance Novels on Par with Porn?" *Huffington Post*, July 31, 2011, http://www.huffingtonpost.com/tag/romance-novels/3, posted 07.31.2011.

9. Christine J. Gardner, "Tangled in the Worst of the Web: What Internet Porn Did to One Pastor, His Wife, His Ministry, Their Life," *Christianity Today,* March 5, 2001, http://www.christianitytoday.com/ct/2001/march5/1.42.html.

10. *Christianity Today,* "Christians & Sex." Quoted in "A Few Scary Thoughts…" *SafetyNet Content Filtering, McG Technologies.* Web, December 7 2009, http://www.mcgtechnologies.net/safetynet/REC/statistics.htm, As compiled by Covenant Eyes, http://www.covenanteyes.com/pornography-facts-and-statistics/, 2011.

11. Sara Gaines, "Why Sex Still Leads the Net," *The Guardian*, February 27, 2002, http://www.guardian.co.uk/technology/2002/feb/28/onlinesupplement.newmedia.

12. Pornography statistics, http://familysafemedia.com/pornography_statistics.html.

13. Ibid.

14. Ryan W. Neal, "Mobile Porn in 2013: Smartphones Most Popular Device for Watching Internet Pornography in US," *International Business Times*, December 23, 2013, http://www.ibtimes.com/mobile-porn-2013-smartphones-most-popular-device-watching-internet-pornography-us-1518868.

15. David McCormack, "Porn study had to be scrapped after researchers failed to find ANY 20-something males who hadn't watched it," *Mail online*, January 12, 2013, http://www.dailymail.co.uk/news/article-2261377/Porn-study-scrapped-researchers-failed-ANY-20-males-hadn-t-watched-it.html.

16. John Freeman, "Sex and the Silence of the Church: How It Is Crippling God's People," *Harvest News,* Fall 2013, Available at www.harvestusa.org, under Learn/Visit our Blog.

17. Dan Allender, "Lust," *Harvest News,* Spring 1998, http://www.harvestusa.org/index.php?option=com_content&view=article&id=429%3Alust&catid=23%3Apornography&Itemid=89&limitstart=1. Accessible through the Learn/Visit our Blog section of the Harvest USA website.

18. John Calvin, *Institutes of the Christian Religion*, Vol. 1, ed. John McNeill, trans. Ford Lewis Battles (Philadelphia: The Westminster Press, 1960), 108.

19. Steven Curtis Chapman and Scotty Smith, *Restoring Broken Things: What Happens When We Catch a Vision for the New World Jesus Is Creating* (Nashville: Integrity Publishers, 2005), 73.

20. "Mr. Thomas Manton's Epistle to the Reader," *The Confession of Faith* (Inverness, Scotland: The Publications Committee of the Free Presbyterian Church of Scotland, 1970), 7.

21. Gerald G. May, M.D., *Addiction and Grace* (San Francisco: Harper & Row, 1988), 3–4.

22. Matthew Zook, "Report on the location of the Internet adult industry," in *C'Lick Me: A Netporn Studies Reader*, ed. Katrien Jacobs, Marije Janssen, Matteo Pasquinelli (Amsterdam: Institute of Network Cultures, 2007), 10321. http://www.networkcultures.org/_uploads/24. pdf, as compiled by Covenant Eyes, http://www.covenanteyes.com/ pornography-facts-and-statistics/ 2013.

23. Frederick Whitfield, "I Need Thee, Precious Jesus," 1855, in *Trinity Hymnal* (Philadelphia: Orthodox Presbyterian Church, 1961), No. 419.

24. Paul David Tripp, "The Way of the Wise: Teaching Teenagers about Sex," *The Journal of Biblical Counseling*, Vol. 13 (Number 3, 1995), 39–41.

25. Martin Luther, *Faith Alone, A Daily Devotional*, James C. Galvin, Gen Ed. (Grand Rapids: Zondervan, 2005), March 8.

26. C. S. Lewis, *Mere Christianity* (New York: The Macmillan Company, 1956), 78.

27. Anonymous, "Effectively Reaching Out When Homosexuality Comes to Church," in *First Steps of Compassion,* ed. David Longacre (Greensboro, NC: New Growth Press, 2009), 7.

28. May, *Addiction and Grace*, 127.

29. May, 168.

30. D. Martyn Lloyd-Jones, *Romans: An Exposition of Chapter 5, Assurance* (Edinburgh: The Banner of Truth Trust, 1974), 31.

31. Ibid., 33–34.

32. Ibid., 41.

33. R. Nicholas Black, *iSnooping On Your Kid: Parenting in an Internet World* (Greensboro, NC: New Growth Press, 2012), www. newgrowthpress.com. Retold as an excerpt from this mini book.

34. May, *Addiction and Grace*, 126.

35. Thomas Watson, *The Godly Man's Picture* (Edinburgh: Banner of Trust Truth, 2007), 230.

36. Ibid., 234.

37. Ibid., 232–33.

38. William Law, *An Humble, Earnest and Affectionate Address to the Clergy,*1761, http://www.passtheword.org/dialogs-from-the-past/address2.htm, Addr. 106.

39. Timothy Keller, "Sowing and Reaping," in *Galatians: New Freedom, New Family*, Sermon preached on May 17, 1998, sermons.redeemer.com/store.

40. Timothy Keller, "The Call to Discipleship," in *The Meaning of Jesus, Part 1: Understanding Him,* Sermon preached on February 9, 2003, www.sermons.redeemer.com/store.

41. Norman Doidge, "Brain scans of porn addicts: what's wrong with this picture?" *The Guardian,* September 26, 2013, http://www.theguardian.com/commentisfree/2013/sep/26/brain-scans-porn-addicts-sexual-tastes?CMP=twt_gu.

42. Arthur Bennett, ed., "Contentment," *The Valley of Vision: A Collection of Puritan Prayers and Devotions* (Edinburgh: The Banner of Truth Trust, 2007), 295.

43. Harvest USA, *Gay: Such Were Some of Us: Stories of Transformation and Change* (Greensboro, NC: New Growth Press, 2009). If you're interested in hearing more of Jack's story and others who left the gay life, be sure and check out this resource.

44. C. S. Lewis, *Mere Christianity* (New York: The Macmillan Company, 1956), 79–80.

45. Scotty Smith, *Everyday Prayers: 365 Days to a Gospel-Centered Faith* (Grand Rapids: Baker Books, 2011), 257.

46. Keller, "The Call to Discipleship."

47. Tim Geiger, "A Helper's Guide to Helping," 2008, Harvest USA unpublished manuscript, 41.

48. David E. Longacre, *Crossroads Group: Choosing the Road to Sexual Purity* (Chattanooga, TN: Turning Point, 2003); Tim Chester, *Closing the Window* (IVP Books, 2010); Harry Schaumburg, *False Intimacy: Understanding the Struggle of Sexual Addiction* (NavPress, 1993), Tim Challies, *Sexual Detox: A Guide for Guys Who Are Sick of Porn* (CreateSpace Independent Publishing Platform, 2010). These are just a few of the many quality resources you can find.

49. Covenant Eyes (covenanteyes.com); NetNanny (netnanny.com); Safe Eyes (internetsafety.com); Accountable 2You (accountable2you. com); Open DNS (opendns.com). These are just a few resources we recommend, and there are many more out there.

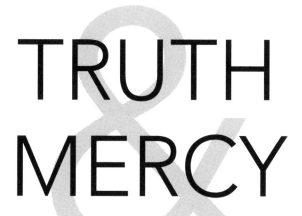

TRUTH & MERCY

Harvest USA brings the truth and mercy of Jesus Christ to men, women, and families affected by sexual sin and equips the church to minister to sexually broken people. We are a faith-operated, missions ministry. Most of our work is given freely or at low cost. We are primarily supported by churches and individuals convinced of our mission.

If you have found this book helpful, consider partnering with us by giving financially, advocating for our ministry in your church, and/or by volunteering your time. For questions, counsel, and opportunities to help, please contact:

Caring for sexually-hurting people in Jesus' name

3901B Main Street, Suite 304
Philadelphia, PA 19127
215.482.0111
info@harvestusa.org
www.harvestusa.org

For Harvest USA resources visit **www.harvest-usa-store.com**
or call 336.378.7775